# A Backpacker's Guide to Making Every Ounce Count

# A Backpacker's Guide to Making Every Ounce Count

Tips and Tricks for Every Hike

STEVEN LOWE

SKYHORSE PUBLISHING

Skyhorse Publishing books may be purchased in bulk at special discounts for sales promotion, corporate gifts, fund-raising, or educational purposes. Special editions can also be created to specifications. For details, contact the Special Sales Department, Skyhorse Publishing, 307 West 36th Street, 11th Floor, New York, NY 10018 or info@skyhorsepublishing.com.

Skyhorse® and Skyhorse Publishing® are registered trademarks of Skyhorse Publishing, Inc.®, a Delaware corporation.

www.skyhorsepublishing.com

10 9 8 7 6 5 4 3 2 1

Library of Congress Cataloging-in-Publication Data is available on file.

Print ISBN: 978-1-63220-694-7
Ebook ISBN: 978-1-63220-955-9

Printed in China

*For my beautiful wife, Andrea, who supports me in all my backpacking adventures. (Or maybe she just wants me out of the house for a week so she can paint another room or rearrange the furniture, again.)*

# CONTENTS

*Did you weigh your toothbrush and sunscreen?*
*Did you cut the tags out of your shirt?*
*Did you forget the TP?*

*"The journey of a thousand miles begins with a single step."*

—Laozi

# INTRODUCTION

How many times have you been backpacking and realized down the road, well, down the trail, that you packed too much stuff or did not pack the right stuff that you needed for the trip? Or worst of all, that you packed everything so quickly that you don't remember where anything is stowed within your pack?

How did your knees and back feel after carrying around so much weight or from an unbalanced pack? What did you learn about backpacking and from whom did you learn these techniques, tips, and suggestions? If there is one thing that I have learned throughout my many years of camping, it's that on each trip I take, I learn something new.

When I first became interested in backpacking, I watched the commercials, and I listened to the store clerks at my local outfitter stores, other self-proclaimed "expert" backpackers, as well as anyone who would talk to me. I listened and ended up carrying so much weight that the trip was not very enjoyable because of how miserable I was at the end of the day.

I hurt. I endured all this discomfort because, even though I carried too much stuff, I wanted to be outdoors. I learned the wrong way to backpack from the wrong people, and I was using bad information. I found myself caught up in the commercialization of the sport and bought the gadgets, the widgets, the wha'chyama-call-its and the do-hickies. I quickly learned that they all had one thing in common: WEIGHT, and a lot of it.

Therefore, I started scouring the Internet, reading books, and watching YouTube videos. I started looking at the items within my pack, as well as the pack itself, and started to change my way of thinking. I learned that there are much lighter options available. Some are DIY, and some are not. I talk about DIY here, but I don't delve too deep into the DIY world, because, well, the DIY world is a big world.

While I was looking for lighter options, I accidentally turned into a Gram Weenie. This book is about how and why I became a Gram Weenie and how a Gram Weenie thinks when preparing for a backpacking trip—at least how I prepare for a trip.

A Gram Weenie, in a nutshell, is someone who is extremely conscious of the weight of every item within their pack.

As you read, you will learn how one Gram Weenie (that would be me) thinks, how to look at the items in your own pack, and how to shave some weight from your pack so you can travel a little bit lighter down the trail. I will also touch on how to pack certain items and how I organize after a trip.

Each backpacker tackles this obstacle a bit differently, so this is not a book on the *only* way to do this or that; this is just the way I do things. You will be able to get a tiny peek into the mind of a Gram Weenie to help you understand how we think, and understand why some folks say the things we do are "crazy," as some call it.

Yes, I cut the tags from my gear and the clothes I wear. Yes, I also cut my toothbrush down so it is shorter; I have been so desperate to shave a few ounces, I drilled holes into the handle of my pot gripper, trying to lose a little bit of weight. (Quick tip: it didn't help.)

I will explain the epiphanies I had and what led me to each one. Learning how I became a Gram Weenie might lead you to your own epiphany or two about your own pack, which will ultimately lead you to a lighter pack.

Once you understand the how and why of thinking the way we do, and you start thinking as a Gram Weenie, you will be making some dramatic changes to your pack, which will in turn lead you to a lighter pack—possibly the lightest pack you have ever carried. You will be looking at your pack from a new and, as some would call it, very weird perspective. But in the end, you will have the last laugh. You will be carrying the lightest pack possible.

Many judge backpackers by the pack they carry. It may be a heavy pack, an old pack, or a really lightweight pack with no frame. But try not to judge a hiker by their pack. Only you can decide what you are willing to carry—either a lot of weight or not a lot of weight. It's just that simple. You basically have two options: light or heavy.

I simply decide to carry as little weight as I can without sacrificing comfort or safety. For me, though, the focus is on comfort, not safety, although I keep safety at a close second. I will use that phrase quite a bit throughout this book because I want to be comfortable, but I do not want to risk my or anyone else's safety. As you read this book, keep an open mind that it is possible to carry a very light pack and still thoroughly enjoy a backpacking trip, without sacrificing either comfort or safety. Once you learn to think this way, you will be able to plan a trip with less or lighter gear.

Good luck, and I hope to see you on the trail sometime.

Steven Lowe

# CHAPTER ONE

# TWO RULES TO UNDERSTAND

I don't have a lot of rules surrounding my gear, but a couple need to be mentioned up front. Rules keep us in line. I know that we are talking about backpacking, but some rules can keep us alive. Every backpacker out there has his or her own rules.

Rule number one is: (Enter your own personal rule number one here.)

There are folks out there who have a list of the items that go into their pack first—on every trip. You may even have your own set of rules you go by while planning for a trip, during the trip, and after the trip.

For me, I keep a few select items in my pack at all times: my knife, headlamp, cook kit, water filter, and a few other items. Right now, my pack is hanging up in my gear closet, but the pack is not empty. There are a few items stowed in the pack ready for my next trip. You know, the stuff that does not need to be maintained other than taking the batteries out of the headlamp.

Some rules can be broken, bent, or otherwise ignored. However, one rule that cannot be argued since it is a fact of science more than a rule is called the Rule of Three.

## The Rule of Three

The Rule of Three has been around since the beginning of time.

The average person, in average situations, can survive about this long:

- Three minutes without air
- Three hours unprotected from harsh elements

- Three days without water
- Three weeks without food

Did you notice the pattern here?

The next rule of Five Cs is an actual rule, and one that I have seen over the years and have adopted on my own trips into the wild. I am not sure who came up with it, but I run across it in many videos online. Folks talk about this rule when discussing their "Bug Out Bag" or their "Get Home Bags," as well as "Bushcraft" and "survivalist" videos and in some backpacking segments. I did not make up this next rule. I've learned this over the many years I have been camping and backpacking as well as during my journey to becoming a Gram Weenie, and I thought it would be something to include here. This is more for your protection and safety should you find yourself in a "Survival Situation."

This rule also applies for those hikers on quick little day hikes. The rule should be honored in every pack out on the trail just due to the nature of each item. If you do not have these items in your small day pack, when you venture out on a hike where "nothing could possibly go wrong," you may find yourself in a world of hurt.

Read the statistic below before reading the rule.

A report from the online journal *Wilderness & Environmental Medicine* has some interesting statistics involving search-and-rescue operations in national parks:

> "From 1992 to 2007 there were 78,488 people involved in 65,439 Search And Rescue incidents. These included 2,659 fatalities, 24,288 injured or sick people, and 13,212 'saves,' or saved lives."

Keep in mind that the statistics above are just for the national parks.

In just this short fifteen-year span, 2,659 folks lost their lives in our national parks. I don't have all the specifics on each incident, but if they were part of a "search and rescue" event, more than likely a large part of those folks got lost or came up missing, which is why they were being searched for and someone was trying to rescue them.

Now you might be saying, "Duh. That's fairly obvious," and you would be right. It is obvious to some. However, the one thing I have noticed during my years camping and backpacking is that some things are not obvious to us until we learn them—usually the hard way.

I would be willing to bet that in the more than 65,000 cases above, each person learned something during their experience. "I wish I had a knife . . . I wish I wasn't so cold . . . I wish . . . I wish . . . " and so on. This may have been due to not knowing, not researching, or simply biting off more than they could chew. It may have been that they had gear with them that they did not test prior to the trip, or they may not have had any gear at all.

Bottom line is to be prepared and do your homework. Knowing the rules is a pretty good start.

The next rule is known as the "Five Cs." You need to have all five of these items in your backpack, Bug Out Bag (BOB for short), or in any day pack because you never really know what might happen out there in the wilderness while hiking.

## The Rule of the Five Cs

- Cover
- Container for water
- Cutting tool
- Cordage
- Combustion device

The above numbers might have been reduced if those folks would have had the items mentioned in the Five Cs with them. The five items listed above need to be in your pack anytime you venture outdoors for a camping or backpacking trip or should you find yourself broken down on the side of the road and having to walk home with your get-home bag.

Not only should you have these items, you also need to know how to use each of them. These items need to be tested prior to going out on a trip. You wouldn't buy a car without taking it for a test drive, would you? You take it for a drive to test the way it handles, the brakes, the radio, the sunroof, or the four-wheel-drive. Same goes with any gear you take with you on a trip—whether it be a day hike or a longer overnight trek.

Think of the 5 Cs as individual pieces of a puzzle, and once you have all the pieces together, and they are in working order, the resulting picture will be you surviving the night should you get lost.

Let's look at each of the items listed in the 5 Cs rule.

## Cover

Extra clothes, rain jacket, a big thick contractor trash bag, or an actual raincoat or wind breaker will do. Basically you need a backup to the clothes on your back should the weather change. It might start raining even though the weather channel said it would be clear all day.

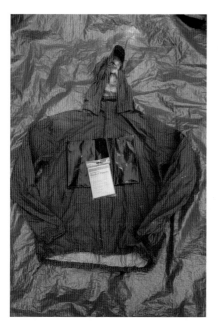

If you are on a day trip up a mountain trail, like the approach trail leading up to the southern terminus of the Appalachian Trail, the weather for Dahlonega, Georgia, (which we use when planning a trip in that area) may not apply to the top of the mountain. Weather changes are quick and unpredictable in the mountains, in the valleys, in the desert, and other places we may want to hike.

I don't want to take a day hike in downtown Atlanta; I want to get away from the city folk, the cars, and other noise. I want to get away, and usually away means to the mountains or some other place not near a town. So having an extra layer will help keep you protected from the elements in case the weather changes unexpectedly.

## *Container for Water*

This is a good one. You need at least one container that you can put over a fire to boil the water within the container, and it should not be made of plastic. However, you can use a plastic container or bag to carry extra water back to camp.

Let's say you are on a day hike, and you get separated from your group or partner because they hike ahead of you. My hope is that you have already discussed this scenario and set the rule that if your group does split up, the hikers ahead will wait at the next intersection, or an obvious stopping point, for the hikers who are a bit slower.

On the other hand, let's say you are out there alone and get lost. You are out of water. You see a stream. You're thirsty. Sure, you can stop to drink, but what about an hour later? Do you have a container to take water with you as you continue to look for a way out?

You will need some sort of container to carry extra water around with you until you can get rescued or find your way back to civilization. Nevertheless, it is usually a safe bet that if you do get lost, you will need to eventually accept the fact that you are lost and stay put.

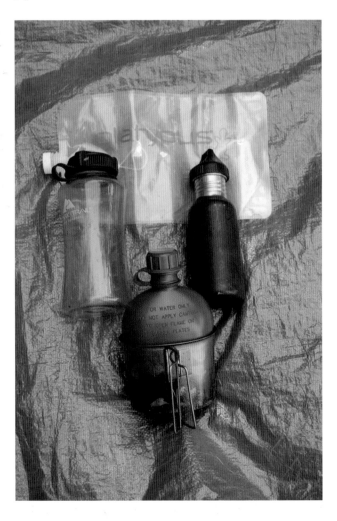

You may already have a container full of water that you brought to keep you hydrated on your "little day hike," but do you have a spare? It might be a good idea to have an empty container with you in your pack. For your spare, it can be a water bag or some sort of aluminum can or bottle. Have at least one container that is made of some sort of metallic material in which you can boil water.

It can be steel, aluminum, or titanium. If you take an aluminum bottle, make sure it is not a double-walled bottle. Only single-walled containers need to go on the fire.

One school of thought is when you go on a hike, you let people know when and where you will be going and what time you will be coming back. If people know you are on a hike, and you do not check in at the right time, calls will be made, and a rescue will eventually get put into motion. You will be found, so stay put. You will be okay because you do have your 5 Cs with you, right?

## Cutting Tool

I carry a knife with me everywhere I go. It is a three-and-a-half-inch long locking blade Winchester that stays in my pocket. For as long as I can remember, I have carried some sort of pocketknife with me. Back in the seventies, I carried a folding Buck knife in a sheath on my belt during camping trips with my family, or a small dual-blade folding knife I used to eat an apple. I have gathered many knives over the years, both folding and fixed blade.

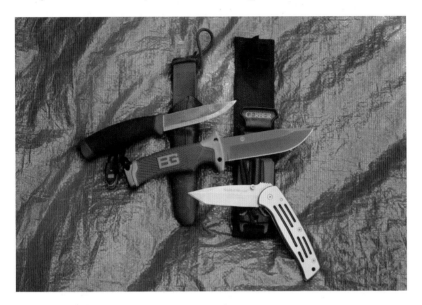

My fixed-blade backpacking knife has changed over the years, but I always have a fixed blade knife with a full tang with me on my trips. The term "full tang" refers to the fact that the metal of the blade extends through the full length of the handle. A knife with a full tang is more stable than a knife that has the tang only extending a few inches into the handle. You need the stability and the durability of a full tang when using the knife to process wood. You may need to "Baton" some wood to make it smaller for the fire. If you take a knife with a full tang and place it at the top of a large diameter stick, you can use another heavy stick and force the blade of your knife down the center of the stick to split the stick into smaller pieces, making it easier to work with and burn.

Why should you carry a knife in your pack? Protection from people or critters? A little pocket knife may not be the best object of defense against a critter or a bad guy because there are usually large sticks on the ground that might work better as a weapon. With a long stick, you can keep some distance between you and the aggressor. Your walking stick would work better if you hike with a trekking pole of some kind.

Nope, the knife is not in your pack for your protection. The knife is there for you to use to build your shelter. Shelter is another one of the Rule of Three, remember? You need to protect yourself from the elements now that you have found yourself lost and in a survival situation.

The knife can help you sharpen the end of a long stick for self-protection should you get attacked. A knife can also allow you to cut vines from trees to help with the lashing of sticks and branches together so you can build a little debris shelter. A shelter will help keep the wind off of you and trap what little heat you are putting off to keep you warm for the night.

You also might need a good fire. Your knife will help you in the processing of the wood needed to build a sustainable fire. You need a knife of some sort to shave bark, cut larger sticks into smaller sticks, and split much larger branches into smaller sticks. A knife can help you dig, or at least shape a flat stick into a trowel-shaped piece of wood that can help you dig.

Hopefully you won't be lost for long, but should you find that you are out there for several days, a knife can help you skin out an animal that you caught with your snares, if your snares are functioning. You need fire to cook the animal and boil water to make it safe to drink. Do you see how it's all starting to tie in together? We're not done yet.

## Cordage

Cordage, in the form of a 550 paracord, is in every kit I have. I have it in my get-home bag that I keep in my truck, as well as in my backpacking gear. I also use 550 paracord as shoelaces on my hiking boots and regular boots. Cordage of some kind is very important to have in any pack.

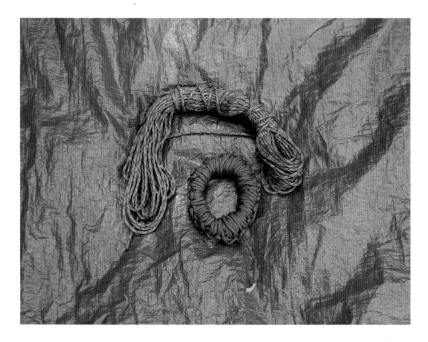

You can use the cordage (here again, I am using 550 paracord as my visual) in many ways if you find yourself in a bad situation on the trail. Paracord 550 is constructed of seven individual strands of continuous cordage.

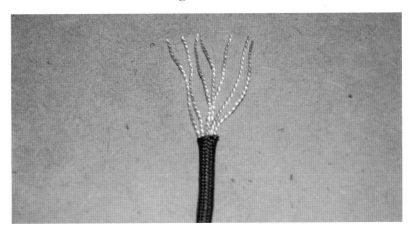

Each of those seven strands is made of two strands, and each of those are made up of very thin strands. All of this is wrapped in a hollow core casing.

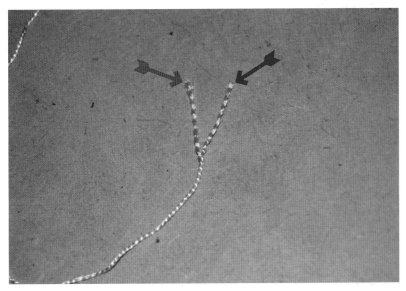

By design, 550 paracord is rated to carry 550 pounds of weight before breaking. I doubt if I would trust this to keep me suspended in a tree at night, but the 550 paracord's many uses will help you survive a bad situation.

You can use paracord as a makeshift sling for an injured arm. You can also use it to lash sticks together to make a sled for an injured person, for a shelter, or to lash gear together to make it easier to carry.

If you separate the strands, you can make a fishing net to trap fish or small snares that can be used to trap small game for food. But you will need a knife to skin out the little critter, sharpen a stick into a skewer, and make fire to cook it.

You can use paracord to repair gear, make a fire bow to build a fire, and in many other ways to help keep you alive while you wait to get rescued should you find yourself lost.

And last but not least, in my opinion, the most important of the 5 Cs: you need some way to make FIRE.

## Combustion Device

Having a combustion device of some kind can save your life, if you know how to take advantage of its full potential. This device can be a disposable lighter or a Ferro rod also known as a fire steel. This little item can really save you in the cold weather that usually comes when the sun drops below the horizon. It will allow you to make fire, which serves several purposes. You may want to also carry along with you some kind of tinder. This can be some dryer lint, or some wax-coated cotton balls, shown in the picture below. If you end up lost in a wet environment, some dry tinder will be nice to have to help get a fire going.

A fire can really boost your mental well-being when lost, and it is a huge morale booster even if you are not lost and safe in a group. A fire has really boosted our morale on many trips. When we were all cold, hungry, and down because of the wind and the freezing temperatures, all our troubles seemed to go away once we got a good roaring fire going. Keep in mind that we were all safe and in a group. Imagine how much having a fire will help if you are alone and lost. We had each other to keep us company and to keep the morale up, but even in a group, without fire, the morale of the entire group can go down in a hurry.

With fire you have the ability to boil water to make it safe to drink, cook food, provide warmth, and protect yourself from critters. You may not see them, but I will bet that they are there just waiting for you to go to sleep so they can rummage through your stuff looking for food.

Now, let's put all five of these items to good use in a possible scenario.

At eleven o'clock one morning John says to his wife, "Honey, I'm going on a day hike up the trail and will call you when I get back to the truck, probably around six or so. I don't want to be out there too late because it is supposed to drop down to about forty tonight."

"Okay sweetie, which way are you going?"

"I will be going north, up the trail."

"Okay, make sure you call me when you get there and as soon as you get back to the truck," she says with genuine concern. "Not a mile down the road once you are warm in the truck, but as soon as you get off the trail and into your truck. Before you even crank it up."

"Okay, I will. Love you."

"Love you, too."

Aww, isn't that sweet? They really love each other. They kiss goodbye, and he is looking forward to the solitude that only the trail can provide him.

John reaches the parking area, calls to check in with the boss, uh, I mean his wife, and starts walking north, just like he said he would.

After about a mile, he finds that the trail has been washed away and covered with large debris. He is there for a simple day hike and does not want to put out the kind of effort it would take to navigate around or over the debris, so he turns around and heads the other direction. He goes south, down the trail, even though he told his wife he would go north. He reaches the truck and continues south but forgets to call his wife and inform her of the change because he is simply just enjoying the walk too much to think about it.

John is not familiar with this trail, so he doesn't know the trail's features or where the water supply is. Nevertheless, it doesn't matter because his plan is to be there for only a few hours.

John hikes and hikes and soon realizes he doesn't see the trail markings on the trees anymore. He doubles back to find his way to the truck but cannot seem to find it where he thought it might be. It is getting late, and he loses sight of the sun, so he then doesn't know which direction he is heading.

It's official: he is lost. He wanders around more but can't seem to find his way and eventually realizes he is heading farther away from the truck than he thought. Or is he? Yeah, he is definitely lost.

It can happen that fast.

The temperature is dropping, so he finally decides to stay put and make the best of it. He looks for his phone to call his wife but remembers leaving it on the seat of his truck. Now he is more afraid of getting into trouble with his wife than of being lost. John feels confident that he would make it through the night because he had his 5 Cs and knows how to use the items. He sits down a while to calm his nerves and starts to evaluate his surroundings, his supplies, and his physical condition.

He hears water running and manages to locate a stream.

Rule of three: Three days without water . . .

He retrieves a container from his pack. He has one that he had been drinking from and one spare, which is made of aluminum, so he can boil the water to make it safe to drink. He fills up both containers and heads away from the water source but stays close enough to get more water later if he needs it.

He uses his knife to cut down limbs and branches and makes a shelter using his cordage to tie it all together. Out of more cordage, he fashions three snares and uses some snacks he has in his day pack for bait, and sets them about a hundred yards from camp with hopes of catching a small animal for food. Once he is happy with the snares, he starts collecting wood for the fire and works his way back to camp. Although he gathers plenty of wood, he looks to ensure he does not run out during the night.

He has a tarp as his cover item from the 5 Cs, so he uses that as the floor of his shelter and, using his disposable lighter, starts a fire.

Rule of three: Three hours without protection from the elements . . .

He uses his **C**over, **C**ontainer, **C**utting tool, **C**ordage, and **C**ombustion device. He is warm, has water, and is able to sleep somewhat comfortably. He is still cold enough to be miserable, but not so cold that he slips into hypothermia. He feeds the fire all night to help keep him warm so he is able to survive the night.

In the morning, he stokes the fire a bit and heads out to find that his snares failed to capture any animals, so no food for breakfast. His bait is gone, so he plans on making the necessary adjustments later. He does, however, still have shelter and water.

He continues to feed the fire that morning, and, since it is daylight, he gathers leaves and brush to burn so someone could see the smoke if they are close enough. He is sure that his wife would have called somebody since he did not return home the night before, so he is preparing a signal to alert anyone that might be near.

Just before lunch, while he is gathering more wood and checking his snares, he hears someone calling his name. He throws the green shrubs and leaves onto the fire to make as much smoke as he can and whistles as loud as he can with three short blasts (the universal signal for help). Someone walks around some trees near his camp. John sees him and calls out, and he's seen by the rescuers.

He is very happy to see these guys and asks the man approaching him, "How did you guys find me?"

"We smelled and saw the smoke from your fire. Then we heard your whistling and followed the smoke." Now this was a quick little story, but you can see how having just a few items and knowing a few other skills can keep you safe until rescued. Just having the equipment, however, is not good enough. Like any equipment in your pack, you need to know how to use it. In the scenario above, John knew how to make a fire, how to lash some sticks together to make a shelter, and how to set snares—even though they failed to catch any critters.

Test your new compass, the new stove, a knife, or your fire-steel. Test from home, folks. I preach this as well as practice it as much as I can. If you have not tested your new gear at home, don't take it with you or depend on it for your survival. I will go over testing from home in Chapter Nine.

But my guess is that you didn't buy this book to learn a bunch of rules. You wanted to learn about how a Gram Weenie thinks. Well, this is how I think when it comes to trying to go light.

Before we get too far down this trail of thinking like a Gram Weenie, understand that the concepts I put forth in this book might sound a bit odd. I've been called crazy, been laughed at and mocked. However, at the end of the trip, I am not nearly as exhausted as I used to be.

Once you learn how a Gram Weenie thinks, you will understand *how* and *why* we think the way we do. It is all about shaving weight from your pack a few ounces at a time. Or since we are called GRAM Weenies, it's all about shaving weight from your pack a few grams at a time. And the ounces or grams do add up.

Here are some figures for you to chew on while you read:

There are 16 ounces (453.592 grams) in a pound. My Soto Micro-regulator stove weighs 2.5 ounces, which is 71 grams.

Or, if you like, think about it like this—if you can shave 4 ounces from four separate items, you have shaved 16 ounces of weight from your pack, which is 1 pound. Sounds good, doesn't it?

If you can shave 100 grams in five areas, that is 500 grams, which is 1.10231 pounds. See how it all adds up? No? Don't worry, you will. You will be switching to the lighter side before you know it.

If you are planning on becoming a Gram Weenie, or at least trying to get a lighter pack, you are going to have to start looking at your pack, as well as the gear inside, a bit differently. You will find other areas where you can shave weight. The tips I offer here are a few ideas. Each backpacker is different, and the gear carried is different, from male to female, state to state, and coast to coast.

I live and primarily backpack on the East Coast, but the philosophy is the same. Look at your gear and try to make it lighter.

Now, let's see who a Gram Weenie is.

# CHAPTER TWO

# UNDERSTANDING WHO A GRAM WEENIE IS

Prior to my first real backpacking experience, I spent a few years camping with one of my fellow backpackers, and we would use our packs even though we were car camping. Car camping is when you drive to a spot, unload all your gear, and camp right there. Some may call it dump camping. Regardless of what you call it, we parked, unloaded, and spent a couple of nights.

We used our packs because it was easy for us to have everything in there that we could haul into camp. At the time, we planned to go backpacking eventually but needed to practice our setup, gear, food, and other techniques. We treated this as testing from home but in the field.

Keep in mind that our car camping excursions involved primitive camping techniques. We would drive into the Chattahoochee National Forest and park the truck. We would still have to carry everything about twenty yards or so, and it was just easier for us to use backpacks.

We usually didn't carry coolers full of food or drink. On occasion, we would carry some steaks and instant mashed potatoes, but mostly we brought dehydrated food and backpacking snacks. We camped near a water source, and we had our filter of choice to make the water drinkable.

Where we camped (and still camp if we need a quick fix) is secluded, near a creek, and just right for about five or six hammocks. Sometimes, my crew and I still car camp there, but it is when we just need a break and need to get out of the house for a quick weekend. I don't like car camping as much as I used to because I have been on enough long-distance trips that I am spoiled. I want to enjoy the walk along the trail. I don't want to spend five minutes walking from the truck to the campsite; I enjoy walking at least six to eight miles to get to the next spot. We are not what you might call distance hikers. We're not out to break any distance records, so we take our time and stop when we feel like it. On the weeklong trips, we do have a schedule to keep, so we make it to the next spot or shelter on time, but we plan these trips so each stopping point is less than ten miles apart. This way, we can enjoy the trip and not wear ourselves out getting to the next spot. We also like to have some daylight left so we can gather wood for fire and set up our hammocks.

For me that is where the fun is. I enjoy the scenery, the sounds, the weather, and everything about the outdoors. For me to car camp now, well, it is not as satisfying as a ten-mile-a-day trip in Virginia, or even a quick three-nighter on the approach trail to Black Gap Shelter and then on to Springer Mountain Shelter.

But back to the story at hand. . . . Both of our packs were over forty pounds when we started preparing to go backpacking. Looking back, I couldn't believe we took some of the things that we took. I mean *come on*! Forty pounds!? Really?

I knew we could do better, so we started evaluating our packs and looking for a lighter way to sleep. We thought about a small one-man tent, a Bivy tent, or anything that was lighter than the three-person, four-season tent I had. We both started looking online and stumbled upon a website. It was like the clouds parted and the angels rejoiced. . . .

(Imitate your own angelic song here. . . .)

The site, *www.hammockforums.net*, is dedicated to backpacking while sleeping in hammocks, and features a ton of DIY tips and tricks for modifying gear and making your own hammocks. My friends and I soon got hooked on hammock camping. I mean hooked big time.

I purchased a "Hennessy Expedition Asym" hammock as soon as I could and thought I was doing better. The hammock slept great once I found my "sweet spot." The setup was a few pounds lighter than my tent, so I felt like I hit the jackpot. Later on I learned how to make my own hammock and sold the Asym to another backpacking buddy. He is a fellow hammock camper and my partner on GaHammockBros.com.

My journey to Gram Weenieism started when I started researching lightweight backpacking. I read books and watched YouTube videos, and read more books and started doing other research online that pointed out the Big Three. If you can get the Big Three down to under ten pounds total, you are getting close to ultralight backpacking. I explain the Big Three in Chapter Three, so keep reading.

This research, and learning new ways to do things, is how I was able to shave fifteen pounds from my original weight of forty pounds. I'm talking about pack weight here, which is everything I will need on a given trip. My base weight, for a three-nighter winter trip now, is under twenty pounds.

The journey to Gram Weenieism does not stop with the Big Three. It all starts with the phrase, Every Ounce Counts. I weigh and count the ounces of everything, trying to figure out what I can cull from my pack.

Think about it in smaller terms and not trying to shave all fifteen pounds at once. If you can pick four areas from your pack, and can shave four ounces from each area, you will have shaved sixteen ounces from your pack. As I pointed out above, there are sixteen ounces in one pound. Once you develop this type of thinking, you will be able to shave some weight from your pack.

If I haven't said it already, I'll say it now, I may be a Gram Weenie, but I am not an ultra-light backpacker. As you read, you will discover the difference. I have learned some tricks and tips over the years, and I will share those tips and some stories, and maybe it will help you to lighten up your pack a little bit. If you slip to the ultra-lightweight side, don't blame me. You are the one who kept reading.

For any type of backpacking, knowing your limitations is crucial. Only you know the level of intensity of terrain you are willing to tackle. You know your friends a lot better than I do, so this is a judgment call where your backpacking partners are concerned.

Once you know your limitations, you will know where and how to cut weight from your pack and other gear to accomplish crossing over to the lighter side of backpacking.

The more time you spend on a task, be it your job or any hobby, the more efficient you will become at performing it. You strive to be better at your job. You want to get the job done in the best way you know how. You learn new travel routes to work to cut down on time in traffic. You learn new software at work, research methods of doing things related to your favorite hobby or projects at home.

The rocky path to Gram Weenieism is no different. If purchasing this book is your first step on that path, I want to take this time to commend you.

Okay, that's enough time, now let's get busy.

As you learn things like cutting your toothbrush in half or cutting the tags off of your clothes, you will also be able to figure out things on your own that you can do to lighten your pack a few ounces at a time—which will add up to a few pounds. The phrase you will hear me say from time to time is, "every ounce counts." This phrase is quite popular to many backpackers trekking up and down the trails. Those backpackers who are true Gram Weenies go by "every ounce counts" with a fervor that would rival a champion hunter on the trail of a record twelve-point buck. He will do whatever it takes to bag the big buck.

More than likely, they probably weigh everything in their packs. They might keep up with the ounces or the grams of every item. They are called Gram Weenies, regardless of the measurement they track—ounces or grams.

The hunter's goal is to bag the big buck, the golfer's goal is to win The Masters, and the ultra-light backpacker's goal is to have the lightest pack possible. I know I said this before, and I am saying it now, and I will say it again . . . they count every ounce of weight. I am not an ultra-light backpacker. I am considered a lightweight backpacker. A Gram Weenie may cut the straps of a backpack and yes, I have cut the straps on my pack to shorten them, and I have cut tags out of my hammocks, pants, and shirts. I don't carry stuff sacks. Well, maybe one, but I keep my sleeping bag in it to protect it from dirt and from being ripped.

If an item does not serve at least one purpose, it is dead weight. I cull these items from my pack and leave them behind, and stuff sacks, in my opinion, are dead weight.

Many items in your pack need to serve at least two purposes, down to your shoe laces. I don't have regular shoe laces. I use 550 paracord that, if needed, I can use to make a fire-bow so I can start a fire. Again, look at Chapter Eleven for suggestions on dual-purpose items.

# CHAPTER THREE

# THE BIG THREE

Years ago, while working in Corporate America, I worked for a company that employed over 7,000 employees worldwide. I remember my supervisor would take any issue and offer three possible solutions. I started paying attention when the second or third issue came up and he offered three solutions. "This is not a big problem," he would say. "You have three choices here on what to do next." He would offer the three choices, and one of them would ultimately lead me to the correct solution each time.

I thought it was odd that there were always three solutions, but there were. It may be that there were more than three, but that was his method.

Likewise, we have three areas to look at to help us reduce some weight from our pack. I ran across this method while on YouTube, and after seeing this more than a few times, I started to take notice. They are the Big Three.

Weight is a big concern for Gram Weenies, and there are two weights on which we concentrate: the base weight and the pack weight.

The Big Three refers to the biggest three items in your pack, other than food. The three largest, if not heaviest, items in your pack are the pack itself, your shelter, and your sleep system.

These three may not be the heaviest items, but they are possibly the largest. On some trips, my food bag is heavier than any piece of gear in my pack.

If you can get the main three items down to three pounds or less, you will be on your way to becoming a lightweight backpacker. Working on getting your big three down in weight might be an ongoing process. Due to financial constraints, I couldn't just go out and get the lightest pack, bag, and shelter I could find all at once. It takes time, and I am still on the lookout for lighter options.

On a week-long trip I took in November 2013, my food bag weighed over eight pounds and five ounces. My pack is an Osprey Exos 58, which weighs in at two pounds, ten ounces, according to REI. Mine weighs a few ounces less than that because I shortened my straps.

You can see how the biggest items may not necessarily weigh the most; however, they are three items that can be reduced down to three pounds or less—with a little work.

## The Pack

The first of the three biggest items in your arsenal is the pack itself.

I used to carry a name-brand pack that weighed over five pounds. It had an internal frame and some internal aluminum reinforcements to provide extra support. The bag itself was made of some heavy canvas-type material, which looked like it would withstand a trip or two up Mount Everest, but it did not have enough volume for a trip of that extent. The pack was seriously too rugged to meet my needs, as I later learned.

On one trip, I actually tried to lighten my load by tearing it down at camp and removing the aluminum struts that were embedded in the main compartment—it didn't help much at all. In retrospect, this was probably one of my first steps down the path to becoming a Gram Weenie; I just didn't recognize it at the time. As I said earlier, the pack and all the gear weighed forty pounds, so I knew I needed to figure out a way to lighten my load. For me, the first logical step was to find a lighter pack.

Several years later, after having learned a bit more, I took a three-night trip to the Smoky Mountains in the winter. I bought an external-frame pack from a local sporting goods store, and the pack might have been defined as a lightweight backpack. The frame was plastic, and the straps were quite adjustable. The pack weighed a little over 4 pounds and 8 3/8 ounces, so I was already 2 pounds lighter.

Unfortunately, the pack broke at Kephart Shelter. I didn't have a burial for the deceased pack because the area that broke is fixable. I can simply add a brace and a couple of small aluminum nuts and bolts, and voilà, it will be back in service. I might use it on some early fall or late spring trips when I don't usually carry a lot of weight. It might not be an ultra-light pack, but it will work on some of my warmer weather trips.

There is a fine line separating lightweight and ultra-lightweight backpacking. The designation actually refers to the base weight, which is all the gear that meets your basic needs for the trip. These nonconsumable items are, but not limited to, your shelter, sleep system, clothes you carry, water treatment, fire-making tools, kitchen equipment, and other items that don't change in weight as the trip progresses. Or if you want to look at it this way, all your gear minus your consumables.

Consumable items are the items that are reduced in weight as the trip progresses, like toilet paper, food, Chapstick [or lip balm], and so on.

Here is a guide to help define the three areas that most folks will look at when deciding in which backpacking category they belong. These base weights are just a guideline to go by:

| | |
|---|---|
| Lightweight | 20–30 lb. |
| Ultra-lightweight | 10–20 lb. |
| Insanity | Under 10 lb. |

Just because you have a four- or five-pound pack does not mean you can't reach lightweight status. Just be mindful of the contents of the pack, and you might still make it. A friend of mine almost accomplished this very thing on a trip up the Approach Trail at Springer Mountain, here in Georgia. His base weight was just over twenty pounds, and this was with a four- to five-pound pack. Remember that this was the weight of his pack without the food, water, and other consumables.

Not long after my Smoky Mountains trip, I went shopping and found the last pack I will ever buy (hopefully).

The Osprey Exos 58 Large, weighing in at two pounds, ten ounces (per REI's description). I think I have a winner. REI.com labels the pack as an "ultra-light backpack." The volume is 3,722 cubic inches (61 liters). This pack is fantastic, but I am not here to give a full review, I am simply telling you about why I selected this to be my primary pack.

The Exos 58 has a thirty-pound limit, which forces me to select lighter gear and fewer items. I didn't want to surpass the thirty-pound limit for my pack weight, so I had to force myself to go down the path to Gram Weenieism.

Force yourself to select a pack with somewhat limited volume, and you will be forced to rethink the rest of your gear. The pack's weight limit helped me lighten my load. Knowing the limits might help you to be more aware of the rest of your gear, which will in turn help you to go lighter.

On one backpacking trip, one of the guys had an eighty-liter pack. I mean it was huge and it was full. Another member of our group told me that he fills the pack up to the limit regardless of the trip. On a summer trip, the pack is full. In winter, the pack is full.

I just don't understand why anyone would fill an eight-liter pack to capacity for a weekend summer trip. This guy is definitely *not* a Gram Weenie. He's a great guy, but he carried way too much weight, in my opinion.

Do not judge a hiker by the pack or the weight of the pack he or she carries. If a hiker wants to carry an eighty-pound pack on a weekend trip, it is that hiker's prerogative.

I was backpacking with a couple of high-school boys of some family friends in Virginia, and we met a hiker who claimed to have been hiking for months. He said he started in Florida and that his ultimate goal was to hit Canada. He was carrying a pack that looked to be as tall as I am, and it was full.

He walked up to us while we were waiting around finishing our snacks and drinking water. He came out of the woods, via the trail, and stopped to talk, but he never took the pack off.

It looked like an older external-frame pack from the seventies. He had what looked like duct tape on the straps and on areas that might have been for small repairs. It seemed clear to me that this pack had seen quite a few miles over the years. He said he would hike until he collapsed each night and pitched his tent on the actual trail. Not a few feet off of the trail, but on the actual trail.

I thought this was a bit disrespectful because some folks do hike well into the night—sometimes because it is cooler. I didn't mention my objection, as I did not know this guy; we were all tired, and I didn't want to start anything that might be confrontational. I figured if what he said was true, he had already been confronted by other hikers on the trail stumbling into his camp.

We talked for a bit, and when we reached the subject of his pack, he got very upset when I asked him how much it weighed. He literally got angry. He gripped his trekking poles tight, his face got red, he raised his voice, and he looked mad. Thinking back, I am glad I didn't mention how it was wrong to camp on the actual trail. There is no telling what he would have done.

He explained how it wasn't anyone's business how much weight he was carrying and then said something that made sense. A lot of sense.

*"If someone wants to carry a hundred pounds, and is able to, and has everything they want or need, it is their business."*

You know, he was right. He wanted to carry the weight, and was able to carry the weight, so he carried the weight. That was his decision.

Try not to get caught up in what everyone else is carrying; make an informed decision and make the best of it on the trail.

His weight probably consisted of many items that he needed for a cross-country hike. Florida to Canada is more than just a stroll in the woods. He probably had a gun in there as well. He may have had more food than I would carry and no telling what else. Basically, since we didn't know his whole story, we were in no place to judge him or his pack.

## Internal, External, and Frameless Packs

You can select your pack from a wide variety of styles, with different kinds of sizes, colors, volume, weight belt or beltless, thin straps or wide straps, straps with and without pads, one main pocket or many pockets, and many more options. However, there are three basic types of packs: those with internal frames, external frames, and packs with no frames at all.

You also may find little day packs, but I doubt you will get much use out of a day pack for a week-long trek. The packs we're talking about here are ones designed for multiple-night or multiple-week treks.

Some of the old-school backpackers years ago, as well as some now, used a pack with an aluminum frame attached on the outside, providing more room inside. They also had anchor points on the outside of the pack to which they attached some gear.

I have seen some bloggers state that they feel a backpacker with gear attached to the outside of their pack signals a newbie. They feel that all gear needs to be inside.

I don't necessarily agree with that statement. I'm not a newbie, and I do have a few strapped-down items on the outside for specific reasons. A motto I go by is planning right and packing light.

Part of planning right has to do with where the gear is stowed away within your pack—or on the outside.

I have a Nalgene bottle on the outside that I do not under any circumstances want inside of my pack. Let me just say that this Nalgene bottle is yellow for a reason. Need I say more? I also have a polyester shirt that I sometimes carry on the outside of the pack, and my Crocs are there as well. Once I have eaten enough food and have made room inside my pack, the Crocs eventually go inside. All three of these items are secured using a shock cord that I have in my pack.

A little side note here: I have a habit of modifying most of my gear when I can to make it more suitable to my needs. I love the DIY aspect of backpacking, and I am handy with a sewing machine and other tools, so when I can modify a piece of gear to customize it, I will. Whichever pack you get, you can always modify it to some degree without jeopardizing the integrity of the pack.

Another item attached to the outside of my pack is my ground cloth, which is a small section of flooring cut out of an old tent. Wrapped up inside the ground cloth, in its own little case we call snake skins, is my rain fly. I keep the tarp here because it protects the bottom of my pack when the pack is sitting on the ground. It is also the very first thing I remove once we get to camp. If the ground cloth gets sacrificed while protecting the backpack, so be it. The material for making a ground cloth is fairly cheap, and I can replace it more easily than my pack.

When I start out hiking, even in the winter months, I wear very little, so the shirt is there should I need to put it on to help me get warm. I keep the shirt on the outside so I can get to it quickly without having to open my pack and dig it out. When I get too warm, I take it off and quickly secure it under the shock cord and keep going. The yellow Nalgene bottle is my "P" bottle.

Once I get to camp, the first thing I do is hang my backpack on a tree with a little sling I made and unfold my ground cloth. Then I take off my boots and put on my Crocs. This is why they are on the outside of the pack. I can put these on quickly to provide my feet a little relief from my hiking boots. I then set up my rain fly that was wrapped up in the ground cloth to get it off the ground. I keep the rain fly packed in the snake skins until the evening.

I then reach in and unpack my hammock and tree huggers. I set that up and then take a break. I lay down for a bit and rest my feet, back, and knees. It feels so great to get some relief from walking all day. At night, I will deploy the rain fly and flip one side over so only one half is staked down. When I get ready to turn in, I flip the one side back and attach the tie-outs to the stakes already in the ground.

Be respectful of others on the trail where you hike. If you have gear on the outside of your pack, for whatever reason, secure it so it doesn't make noise. One of the reasons I go backpacking is to get away from the noise and enjoy the serenity of the outdoors.

Let's take a brief and maybe obvious look at the pack types.

The external framed pack is a good pack, and you can attach items to the frame, as I described above, and yet still have plenty of room inside. The goal is to pick a pack that is comfortable and meets your needs for the trips you will be taking, and it needs to hold all your gear. Be mindful of the total volume of the pack. Your pack of choice needs to be big enough to carry all your items, and this may be a trial-and-error process until you have been on a few trips and become more familiar with your gear and how much volume is required inside the pack.

Here is a pack I bought from a local sporting goods store, which has the design of the old school pack, but with a plastic external frame.

The pack's frame is adjustable to accommodate several sizes and body types. This is the pack that broke on me while on a trip in the Smoky Mountains. I will eventually repair it and use it as a spare or maybe use it on some trips during the warmer months.

You may find, as I do, that external-framed packs tend to carry differently from internal-framed ones or packs that are frameless. You may want to go to your local outfitter and pick out different types, load them up with gear, and walk around the store for several minutes. This will help you see how each pack type sits with your body type.

However, in my opinion, the first thing to consider is the pack's weight when empty, before you determine the volume you need. You are after all trying to go light, right? You may also find that an internal-frame pack and an external-frame pack of the same volume will vary in weight. I suggest you spend a lot of time when picking out your pack. Packs can get expensive, and it would be a bad thing to spend most of your money from your backpacking fund on a pack only to get out on the trail and discover that you made a mistake. I went through two other packs prior to landing on my Osprey Exos 58. I may get another pack one day, but for now, this is my pack of choice.

The internal-framed pack is just what it sounds like—the frame is inside the pack. Most internal-frame packs that I have seen have D-rings or loops and straps available to let you attach small gear. You may want to attach a dirty pair of shoes, or even a little yellow bottle, or wet gear to the outside so you don't dirty up the inside. My Osprey has a stretchy pocket with a drain hole at the bottom specifically designed to hold wet gear, a feature I love. This is where my raincoat rides.

I have seen some through-hikers starting their long trek at Springer Mountain Shelter line their packs with the large construction-grade black trash bags. One guy used a large trash compactor liner for his pack. This protects the inside of the pack from dirty gear and keeps the gear dry if it rains. When I asked why he had an inner bag as well as a waterproof pack cover, he stated that he was through-hiking up the Appalachian Trail and wanted the extra protection. With the liner inside the pack, and the pack cover, he was confident that the gear as well as the pack were protected from getting wet.

Frameless packs don't have any frames. The design makes them strong enough to carry all your gear without the need for a frame. Some of these frameless packs are super light, and some even have external pockets for some of your lighter or smaller gear.

When selecting a pack, get some help from the folks at your local outfitter so you can be fitted with the right size, style, and type. Explain all your needs to the associate so they can point you in the right direction. Just make sure the weight of the pack is what you are looking for. Ensure that the volume and the weight limit are acceptable as well. You may have other considerations that I might not be aware of, so you can add those to the list as you see fit, but since our goal is to have the lightest pack possible, regardless of the pack you select, you will still be able to remove a few ounces from the pack.

## Packing Your Pack

Typically, there are a couple of theories on how to pack. Some say to load all the heavier items near the middle, closest to your body, to help with maintaining your "center of gravity." This is what I do. I load my sleeping bag in the bottom and stuff all my soft gear—like my hammock, spare clothes, and bug net—down in the corners around the larger bulky items. My stove and fuel go on top, as well as my food bag, which is the heaviest item in my pack starting out.

This is my method. I have spoken with the guys at my REI store, and they told me that women need to pack differently. I am not sure about this, so research how to load your pack. Ask yourself if you are comfortable with the load.

During my SCUBA diving days, we used the phrase "comfort and fit" when deciding which gear to buy. Did it fit correctly and was it comfortable to wear? I would say that the same goes for backpacking gear, especially your pack. If the pack is not comfortable, and you are planning a trip that is to last the weekend or even a week or longer, you will have a very bad trip. Please don't get into the mindset of "I will get used to it." If you take that chance, you may regret it.

Once you have selected your pack, you may be able to shave a few ounces from it to help it be a little bit lighter.

## *Shelter*

The second of the Big Three is your shelter.

Staying out of the weather, whether it is the rain, snow, hot sun, or wind, is a top priority when on the trail. A dependable shelter, in my opinion, is the most important item to have in your pack—next to your knife, lighter, water purification system, sleeping bag . . . okay, okay, it is all very important. That is the thing with backpacking: if something is not important, it is unnecessary, so you may not need to pack it. More on luxury items in Chapter Five.

A good shelter will protect you from the elements. You may have seen the survival shows where the survivalists built a shelter as soon as they could before the sun set. In the show where they were in a wet environment, they needed to get out of the water and dry, so they headed to higher grounds or to the trees. In the desert, they had to be off the ground because of the creepy crawlies like scorpions or snakes and tried to find some shade there. In the snow-covered areas, they built snow caves to protect themselves from the bitter wind and cold.

Rule of Three . . . the average person, in average situations, can survive about three hours unprotected from the elements.

If you are not protected from the elements while on the trail, your trip will be very uncomfortable to say the least. There are three primary shelters you might see other backpackers using. Depending on your comfort zone, you will need to make your decision about which shelter type is best for you once you have more information.

Regardless of which shelter you select, you will need to keep a few things in mind. They are without a doubt, price, as well as comfort, level of protection, and of course, weight. The primary goal for a shelter is to protect you from the wind, rain, and temperature. You have to ask yourself what you want out of a shelter as far as weight, style, and comfort. If you're thinking about going as light as possible, I would say that style might not be at the top of your list of priorities.

Which is more important to you, comfort or safety? Or do you want the same shelter everyone else is using? I don't care about anybody else. If someone has a shelter that I like, and it is light, and comfortable, and can keep me warm, I might consider it as my next shelter. However, I don't just go out and get something because it is the next best thing out there. Safety is not my biggest concern. Now follow along here and let me explain. We are back-packing, so for me, weight is at the top of the list, coupled with comfort. The safest way to camp, in the safest shelter possible, would be to stay at a hotel, and that is not my definition of camping. I mean how safe can you really be, wrapped up in a thin piece of tent material, hammock, or out in the open lying on a tarp? I want comfort and light weight.

Do you want heavy, light, or ultra-light? Or an easier question to ask is this: do you want to sleep on or off of the ground? I am a little biased here because I prefer the hammock, but more on that later. Let's first look at the shelter options more closely.

## Tents

My wife bought me a four-season Kelty tent that weighs eight pounds, and I love it. I have used it on several occasions when she goes camping with me, but I don't like carrying a tent around and sleeping on the ground. That would mean I would have to take an air mattress or some sort of pad to sleep on. The forest floor can be rough on the back, and let's face it, all that extra stuff means extra weight. I can't carry around too much weight and follow the philosophies of Gram Weenieism.

There are some lightweight and reasonably priced tents out there if you look hard enough. You can opt for a dome tent or an A-frame tent, which are both good and each have their pros and cons. They also may even weigh a lot less than my four-season tent. If you choose a larger tent, for two or more campers, you will need to look into sharing the load, which I cover in Chapter Thirteen.

Here are a few of the pros that go along with camping in a tent:

- You share the load with a fellow hiker who will also be sleeping in the tent.
  - At night, you can store all your gear in the tent so it stays drier and warmer than if you stored it outside.
  - You have the privacy for when you need to change clothes or when nature calls. And for this, tents are great.
  - Your tent becomes a nice tight little storage unit with you and all your stuff.
- However, you also have some cons as well:
  - You need to find a level area that is clear of roots, sticks, and rocks before you can set up a tent.
  - You have to sleep on the hard, cold ground or carry padding to sleep on.
  - You run the risk of getting wet if a rainstorm rolls in, so if the weather looks questionable, you will need to look for a higher spot to pitch your tent. I have had this experience, and it is not a fun one. It added to the memories of the trip, but we were miserable, and it took way too long to dry out all the gear.

# Hammocks

Since I am a hammock camper, this is my preferred way to sleep. Imagine sleeping on a fluffy cloud—I feel like I'm sleeping on a cloud every time I hit the trail. My hammock and rain fly weigh four pounds and five ounces, which doesn't quite make my Big Three limit.

I have several combinations of hammocks. I have a Clark Jungle hammock (my newest and favorite one), two Eno hammocks, and a few DIY hammocks. I sleep comfortably and I'm warm, but more importantly, the hammock is light. I don't carry tent poles (the Clark has two very tiny poles that weigh very little). I don't carry any kind of air mattress either—just me on a cloud. After a long day of hiking, my hammock is the first thing I set up. Then I kick back and rest a little while swinging back and forth like on a little swing. A hammock is great for sleeping, but some can set it up like a chair. Ground dwellers (those who sleep in a tent) can't do this.

Here is a shot of my Clark.

When ground dwellers lie down to rest after a long day of trekking through the woods, they are on the hard ground, even if they have an air mattress or foam pad. It is just easier for me to get in and out of my hammock than to crawl in and out of a tent.

Also, after bending over and picking up wood to build a fire, and other camp activities, my back hurts by the time I finally turn in. However, in the morning, after having slept on, well . . . basically

I sleep on air, I have no back pain. Why, you might ask? That's a good question. I have three words for you.

No pressure points.

In a hammock, you don't have anything pushing against your back, so your muscles can rest without any resistance. Sleeping in a hammock is so nice once you find your sweet spot. In some hammocks, you sleep in a slight diagonal position, off center with the foot end slightly elevated so when you do find your sweet spot, you actually sleep level. In my Clark, I don't sleep in a diagonal, I sleep straight and level.

However, this is not a book on hammock camping. I want to talk about going light, and a hammock is quite a bit lighter than a tent (depending on the tent you select). You might be able to find a two-man tent that weighs less than my hammock setup, so keep looking. I don't carry my hammock in a stuff sack. The Clark and the Eno both come with a stuff sack built into the body of the hammock, but in my pack, I simply stuff the loose hammock in and around my other gear, filling in the open corners within the pack. Because of this, my hammock takes up very little room.

I don't need any hardware with my setup either. I don't use any carabiners for the hammock or the rain fly. So again, no wasted weight. My suspension is a one-inch-wide length of webbing that holds my whoopee slings—no knots. I use a Bowline knot on one end of my rainfly line, but even under a lot of tension, the Bowline knot is easily untied. Everything else is a whoopee sling made out of 3/8-inch amsteel. The Bowline knot is in fact a knot, but unties easily, and the rest of my setup does not have any knots; I call it a no-knot setup.

Even though the hammock is much lighter than some tents, there is an even lighter option.

## The Tarp

Some true ultra-light backpackers may be thinking that a tarp is the lightest thing out there, and they would be right. When you sleep, you can fold the tarp in a way that part of it is above you acting as your rain fly.

Some hammock campers use an oversized rain poncho, which serves as a dual-purpose item. The poncho acts as a raincoat for the hiker when it rains and a tarp when the backpacker sleeps on the floor. Not for me.

The tarp can be set up quickly in case a rain storm should sneak up on you. For now, just know that you have an option to lightening your pack by sleeping in something other than a tent. If you don't mind sleeping on the hard, cold forest floor, go with a tarp. You can find several ways to set up a tarp in such a way to keep you somewhat dry.

You have some of the same cons with a tarp as you do with the tent:

- You still need to find a flat area with nothing poking up, and find high ground if it should rain.
- A tarp is less secure when it's raining since you have two open ends and maybe more, depending on how you set it up.

- Since your tarp doesn't come with a bug net, you run the risk of cold critters, both animals and insects, climbing into your sleeping bag with you, trying to get warm. In the warmer months, don't forget about snakes.

While sleeping on a tarp, some hard-core ultra-lightweight backpackers sleep on their clothes or their pack as a pad, which also provides insulation. That seems a bit too bulky for me as well.

A true Gram Weenie would probably opt to use a tarp for a shelter. Since I don't have the back for sleeping on the ground, or enjoy hearing my bones sounding like a breakfast cereal in the morning, I opt for sleeping in a hammock with a rain fly. If your goal is to convert completely to Gram Weenieism, and become an ultra-light backpacker, the tarp may just be your choice of shelter on the trail.

The tarp is light and can be rolled and stored outside of your pack so it will not take up any room inside. Setting up a tarp is quick, and there are several ways to do it.

Let's say that you're on the trail, and the rain slows down your gait, but you decide to keep on hiking. Then you hear the clap of thunder rolling in from the north. You see the clouds darken, and then your inner instinct yells so loud that your fellow trekkers even hear the taunts. "Take shelter! *Now!*"

You can set the tarp up in a quick-mode style:

Your tarp, some cordage that you have (remember the 5 Cs), and your trekking poles are all you need. You can have your tarp set up in no time while others are still trying to find a flat piece of dirt and fit their tent poles together. Either that, or they will be hunkering down and waiting out the storm under your tarp. Which is fine, so don't get me wrong. When on the trail, another thing to remember is it's important to take care of your own needs while also being willing to help others when they struggle. We are all on the same team with the same goal: to experience God's creation in its raw natural form. If one member of the team suffers, the whole team suffers, so help out where you can, when you can, as much as you can.

### Sleep System

The third item of the Big Three is your sleep system. Sleeping bags and a sleeping pad, or for the hammock campers, an underquilt (for the colder trips), make up your sleep system. If you are in a tent, your sleep system will be what you sleep in and/or on.

I opt for the underquilt and no pad for my hammock because after sleeping on a pad inside of a hammock, I found that the pad had a habit of slipping out from under me and my backside got cold. You don't want a cold tushy when you are camping.

An underquilt, in its simplest description, is a unit that hangs underneath your hammock and insulates your backside from the cold.

The underquilt can be another sleeping bag or a down quilt, or even made out of another material like Insultex. I have even seen pictures of hammock campers using their down coat as an underquilt, also known as "UQ," which makes their down coat a dual-purpose item.

Here is one of my old sleeping bags I modified to be used as an underquilt, shown with one of my ENO hammocks.

Right now I use a DIY underquilt made out of Insultex along with my down sleeping bag, and I stay quite warm. My sleeping bag and UQ weigh in at 3.99 pounds. DOH! I missed it that time, too, didn't I?

So, for my three big-ticket items, I have this much weight:

Pack: 2.79 pounds
Shelter: 4.34 pounds
Sleep system: 3.99 pounds

Grand total for the Big Three: 11.12 pounds. Wow, I almost made it. My ultimate goal is to get the total down to ten pounds or less. I may even cut my underquilt down to a two-thirds quilt or even in half. It's a journey, becoming a Gram Weenie, but we have only just begun . . . began . . . which is it? Well, like we say in Georgia, we're just gettin' started, folks.

So how can you lighten your load with your sleep system? Well, since your sleeping bag is the primary item of your sleep system, let's start there. Without a doubt, your synthetic bags will be heavier than their down counterparts.

You can go with a wool blanket, which is by far the best way to go since wool will keep its insulation value even when wet. But who wants to lug around a wool blanket?

Your typical down sleeping bag can weigh around a pound or up to three pounds depending on which brand you choose. While researching sleeping bags for this book, I found a synthetic "Big Agnes" rated for +15° (F) and a Down "Sierra Designs" rated for +13° (F) that were the same size—they were both listed as "regular."

The Big Agnes weighs three pounds four ounces (fifty-two ounces) and costs $169.95, and the Sierra weighs one pound fifteen ounces (thirty-one ounces) and costs $499.95. The two bags are similar in rated temperature, and you can see the difference in weight—you do the math.

Moreover, since the Sierra is down, it will be more compact than the Big Agnes. More down means more "fluff," which also means it will be more heavy. The fluff is where you get your insulation.

Regardless of the bag you get, the less you wear while in the bag, the warmer you will be. I know it sounds crazy, but it is true. Try it, you might be surprised.

Several years ago I went on a trip in the Smoky Mountains, where we spent our last night at Ice Water Spring Shelter. The shelter was on top of a bald (a mountaintop without trees), and it was very windy that night.

Because there were very few trees around the shelter, it got very cold. Our thermometer told us it got down to 5°F. I have no idea what the wind chill was, but, Da-gum, it was some kind of cold that night.

I slept in my REI Halo, which is rated to +25°F. You would think I was cold, but like I stated earlier, I slept in very few clothes. Once I got into my sleeping bag, I stripped down to my base layer and stored my fleece as the bottom layer and put my pants at my ankles.

I used my shirts as a pillow and zipped myself up tight. The only thing that was exposed to the outside air was my face. We slept in a shelter, as per regulations, which helped with the wind, but it was still cold. Up in the Smoky Mountains, they do not allow camping in tents, so we had to use the shelters.

In the middle of the night, nature called. I couldn't just stand up in the shelter and use my yellow Nalgene bottle because of all the other campers, so I had to get up and get dressed and walk to the wood line to take care of my business. I slipped my shirts on and started fighting with my pants.

I was so snug in my sleeping bag, it was harder to get my pants on than it was to take them off. Without thinking, I unzipped the bag all the way down and then it hit me. The five-degree plus wind-chill hit me like a backhoe, and I started shivering uncontrollably. I was on the edge of hypothermia and I knew it.

When you get cold, your body starts to shiver and tries to raise its core temperature. Shivering and shaking generates heat, and this is a defense mechanism built into our bodies to survive when the temperature drops. We all shiver occasionally, but we are able to get warmer again, and the shivering stops.

The thing is, I could not stop shivering. I had all my clothes back on, which included my base layer, a layer of fleece, my pants, a shirt, and my down coat. And I still could not stop shaking. I climbed out of my bag, closed the bag, and headed to the woods. Trying to answer the call of nature in the middle of a cold night is tough enough. Try it when you can't stop shaking.

Once I finished my business, I ran back to the shelter and stripped back down to my base layer shaking so violently I honestly thought I was going to lose my dinner—rehydrated spaghetti, meat sauce, and a Snickers bar.

Once in my bag, again wearing very little, I was warm in only a few minutes. I was so thankful I had my down sleeping bag that night.

The thing to remember about a sleeping bag is to go with down if your checkbook will allow. Down keeps you warmer and is very compressible, unlike synthetic bags.

I use a simple stuff sack with my sleeping bag because I want to protect it from other gear in the bag, but I don't, as a rule, use stuff sacks for any of my fabric-based gear like my hammock or bug net. I use sacks for gear like food and personal items. When you use a stuff sack for your hammock, tent, rain fly, or other fabric-type gear, you create pockets within your pack allowing for dead air space.

My stove, shoes, food bag, and personal kit are bulky items that create dead air pockets throughout my pack. I use my clothes, hammock, and bug net to fill in those dead-air pockets. This way, I am able to use every cubic inch of my pack, which could, if I let it, allow me to take more gear. For me, dead-air pockets are just as bad as dead weight. Because my sleeping bag is in a stuff sack, not a compression sack, it becomes flatter as the weight of the other gear is loaded into the pack.

This is one trick I use when I pack. This allows me to get more gear in the bag and fill in some of the unused open spaces created by more bulky items like my stove. I could just stuff my sleeping bag down into my backpack without the stuff sack, but then I would be exposing the bag to the possibility of getting damaged or dirty.

Hopefully the tips on the Big Three have helped you reduce your weight a bit, and you now have an idea of how we think, so do you want to go further?

I thought you might. What kind of backpacker are you, or what kind do you want to strive for?

# CHAPTER FOUR

# WHAT TYPE OF BACKPACKER ARE YOU?

You're now starting to understand what a Gram Weenie is and how to look at three major items in your pack to lighten some weight. Now, it is time to ask yourself a few questions:

- What kind of backpacker are you or do you want to be?
- Do you want a lighter pack?
- Do you want to change what you carry?
- How far will you go to get the lightest pack you have ever had?
- Are you willing to suffer through the mocking and ridicule that comes with making the changes you are about to start making?

To determine what type of backpacker you are (lightweight or ultra-lightweight), you need to look at the base weight of your pack.

When weighing your setup to determine if you are nearing the rank of light or the ultra-light backpacker, you need to look at your base weight. Here is the table again with the three ranges to refresh your memory:

| | |
|---|---|
| Lightweight | 20–30 pounds base weight |
| Ultra-Lightweight | 10–20 pounds base weight |
| Insanity | Under 10 pounds base weight |

## Base Weight

The base weight is the weight of the pack, loaded with all your gear for a trip, minus the consumable items. Consumable items are the items that change weight during your trip, like your toothpaste, TP, sunscreen, food, fuel, and so on. Items to include when weighing your pack for the base weight are those that do not change weight during your trip, like your pack, sleep system, shelter, stove, clothes, tools, tent stakes, toothbrush, and the like.

Some may say that if the base weight of the pack is less than tweny pounds, then you have an ultra-light pack. Therefore, if you try to get the Big Three down to three pounds each, you might have slipped over to Gram Weenieism because you are taking those steps. I know this because you worked hard to limit the weight of the three biggest items in your pack. Well done!

Pat yourself on the back. . . .

Since the terms lightweight and ultra-lightweight refer to the total weight of your pack with your nonconsumable items, it is conceivable for you to reach light or ultra-light status with a five-pound pack as well as with a three-pound pack. You can find packs that weigh in the one- to two-pound range, so if this is what you are looking for, use the Internet to find the lightest pack possible.

Even though REI calls my Exos an ultra-lightweight pack, I don't agree with that description. The Exos weighs in at two pounds, ten ounces (that is one of the big three here), and that is way heavier than other packs I have found that weigh only a few ounces, up to one pound and slightly over, but not more than two pounds.

You might be able to see how opinions differ from what one person calls an ultra-light pack and a lightweight pack. Some may call a base weight of twenty-five pounds ultra-light because they are used to a forty-five-pound base weight pack. The designation of lightweight backpacker and ultra-lightweight backpacker is subjective.

I looked at these "ultra-light" packs, which are frameless, but I am not thrilled with the idea of a frameless pack. I have noticed that some packs have changed over time. As you take your journey down the path to becoming a Gram Weenie, you will also see changes in pack design, weight, style, and some that go from frame to frameless. So keep an eye on the industry and watch as trends change, which they will from time to time, so you can change with the times, or at least know what is out there to help you make your decision. This goes for packs, stoves, sleeping bags, and other gear.

Remember, I am a Gram Weenie, but I am not an ultra-light backpacker. I know, I've said that before. The path to Gram Weenieism has many twists and turns. As you travel, you will learn new information that will help you to look at your gear in a way that allows you to shave even more weight from your pack. One day there might be some gear out there that is lighter than what I have and get me to the ultra-lightweight side of backpacking. For now, however, I will remain on the lightweight side of the spectrum.

A Gram Weenie can still be someone who carries around thirty pounds for a base weight, it just so happens that this particular Gram Weenie has a lot of stuff in his or her pack. What is the gear in their pack? What effort was taken to use the lightest possible gear? How many luxury items are in the pack?

## *Pack Weight*

The pack weight is the weight of the pack with everything in it, including your consumables. Remember that consumables are those items that are reduced in weight throughout the trip. I have actually culled my deodorant from my pack because I didn't use it, and then put it back after a few trips where I did need it. Well, the other hikers appreciated the fact that I took my deodorant on the trips in the warmer months. Weather conditions dictate when I take my deodorant along.

When trying to go light, the items within the pack are just as important as the pack itself, but when you start the journey to Gram Weenieism, as any journey you take, you must not sacrifice your health or safety. This is very important. If you have special medical needs, you can't cull those items from your pack. However, you can cut back on the amount of TP that you . . . oh wait, NOOOOOO, DO NOT CUT BACK ON THE TP! Trust me on this one.

After testing from home, you can take only the right amount of fuel, only the number of snacks you can eat day to day, and a few other things I will cover as you read on. Hopefully you have learned the difference between a lightweight backpacker, like myself, and an ultra-lightweight backpacker. Now, you have to decide which one you are and/or want to be.

You need to keep that in mind as you read, because knowing what goal you want to accomplish will spur ideas of your own on how you can adjust your pack to meet your needs. It's like a seed that needs nourishment and care. The seed here is ultra-light or lightweight. The nourishment and care are the ideas here and the ideas that you come up with on your own and learn as you make your own journey to Gram Weenieism.

Now, let's take a close look at some other areas you can focus on to lighten your pack a little. Remember, every ounce counts. You will be able to lighten your load more than you dreamed possible.

Some of my friends that I go backpacking with have given me a hard time about some of the things I do when preparing for a trip. However, that same group of people have adopted some of my practices, and have asked me about ways to lighten their packs. Some are also still carrying a heavier-than-needed pack on these trips, while I carry much less. Because I carry less than I used to, I find the trip more enjoyable because I am not as sore or tired as I used to be. At the end of each day, I seem to have more energy than the others, which is good on those trips when I drive us to the trail. If I am not as worn out as other hikers, I don't mind the drive as much. I also try *not* to carry any superfluous items.

# CHAPTER FIVE

# LUXURY ITEMS

Your luxury items are anything you want to take that does not meet the regular pack criteria of dual-purpose items, shelter, sleep, clothes, or food. You know, the things that you actually need to survive the trip. The luxury items serve one, and only one, purpose: to make your trip more comfortable.

Choose your luxury item(s) wisely. I recommend only one, but if you are willing to carry the extra weight, carry as many as you want—or none at all. For me, my luxury item is my small compact radio.

- Is it necessary? Absolutely not!
- Is it dual-purpose? Absolutely not!
- Is it heavy? Well, it's not too bad.

However, another item that might be considered a luxury item is my coffee maker with drip-style coffee. I do like my coffee and a lot of sugar. Yes, I like my coffee sweet. On a three-day trip, I carry about eight ounces of coffee and sugar with me. I know . . . it's a lot of weight, but I have to have my coffee in the mornings. I have to carry around coffee, sugar, and some sort of insulated cup. I don't actually need it in the morning, and I can survive the back-packing trip without my coffee—it doesn't have a dual purpose; it is simply dead weight.

Oh, but to wake up at the crack of dawn and listen to the world waking up is hard to put into words. I can listen to the sounds of crickets and other critters dancing through the woods to the songs of the early birds. I enjoy watching the morning fog being burned off by the rising sun, and listening to the cracking and popping of the fire while I am sipping on my coffee. It's a great part of the trip for me. Having my morning coffee while backpacking is one of the things I simply enjoy. I am usually not a coffee drinker here in civilization, but during hunting season, traveling in the early mornings, and backpacking is when I enjoy it most.

My morning routine actually starts the night before.

At night, before we all turn in, I stack some small twigs and dry leaves into a pile near the fire-pit. I also gather other sticks no larger than a cigar in a separate pile. In the morning, I roll out of my hammock, and after my morning latrine trip, I stoke the fire with the small pile of twigs and leaves.

While it starts to smoke up, I crank up my stove and start to boil water. Next, I place more of the small twigs, already piled up waiting for me, into the fire-pit and stir the ashes up to locate some still-smoldering embers from the previous night's fire. When they start to smolder and smoke, I blow the coals into a flame and add some of the larger twigs to the pile until I have a nice little fire going. Usually, by this time, my water is boiling, and I fix myself a nice cup of Joe.

Keep in mind that it is still dark out (usually), and by the time the fire is self-sustaining, I can enjoy my coffee around the little campfire, and I am able to enjoy the sunrise. While the fire is smoldering, one of my backpacking partners, Josh, usually wakes up and joins me.

Also, the fire is a wake-up call to the others in our group for when they finally roll out of their hammocks or crawl out of their tents complaining about an aching back. The other campers are very thankful Josh and I are early-risers and pyros. Yeah, I like to build the fires on our trips.

But back to the radio as my luxury item. Mike, another one of my backpacking partners, likes to take his compact radio along in case I don't take mine. The entire group likes to listen to it in the afternoon. I do carry the extra weight, but since the entire group can enjoy the music, it is worth it in my mind.

You might want to take along a good book, or a deck of cards, or maybe even a flask of your preferred libation—for medicinal purposes only I'm sure.

I guess the point here is that since you have to carry the weight, and you want to enjoy the trip, take whatever you want. Nevertheless, remember that every ounce counts, and you will be the one carrying the extra weight.

Look at your pack's contents one item at a time and ask if you need this item for any one of the following:

- Eating
- Sleeping
- Water purification
- Shelter
- Security
- Personal hygiene

You are basically asking if you actually need the item. If you really do not need the item to survive, you don't need to take it.

Notice I harp on the word "need." Growing up we always had everything we needed. Maybe not everything we wanted, but my dad made sure we had everything we needed.

Gram Weenieism follows this rule of thumb as well. As a Gram Weenie who weighs everything, you have to ask yourself if what you are taking is something that you really need.

There is a lot of cool gear out there to make your life more comfortable out on the trail, but as you go, the more trips you take, the more miles you have under your feet, the more experience you get while backpacking, you may find that you will cull many items from your pack.

The more guilty pleasures you can cull from your pack, the lighter it will be. Better yet, the more items you can replace with smaller, lighter, and dual-purpose items, the lighter your pack will be. So get rid of most, if not all, of those guilty pleasures and lighten your load some. I could take the instant coffee, which is lighter, and as the trip progresses, lose some of the weight each morning, but real coffee tastes better than instant.

Sure, I can and have eliminated the coffee maker, and I take way less coffee in the instant form instead of the drip kind. The weight of my coffee maker remains constant throughout the trip, so after I use the coffee maker on the final morning, that weight becomes dead weight. When it comes to my coffee, the weight is in the coffee and sugar. My coffee maker is a solid piece of plastic that holds a filter and weighs only an ounce and a half.

You may not need the guilty pleasure items as much as you think you do. So get rid of them. I would be willing to bet that you have certain items that you take on each trip. I also would bet that on many of the trips you take, with said items, you did not use the items at all. Cull them while it is still not too late.

Otherwise, just be able and willing to carry the weight on each day of the trip. One guy I know carries his little iPod preprogrammed to play for an hour at night and with the earbuds in his ears, he drifts off to sleep. After an hour, the iPod shuts off. He says it helps him sleep.

I take ear plugs to block background noise because some of the fellas I go with snore like chainsaws. I do too, but I have never heard myself snore. My little ear plugs only weigh an eighth of an ounce.

Every ounce counts.

# CHAPTER SIX

# FOOD BAG AND OTHER KITS

Watch one hour of your favorite television show. How many commercials were about some sort of food? How many were for snacks, prepackaged meals, or restaurants? What about some sort of drink like an energy drink or even coffee? A lot of our culture is food-based because we spend quite a bit of time eating. The trail is no different.

Another big area where you can pile on the weight is with your food. Since we love to eat, and since you need quite a few calories each day to give you the energy to tackle a big trip, you need to take along a lot of food. The food needs to, and can, be light.

Now I am not going to get into a long drawn-out chapter here, so for detailed nutritional facts, talk to your doctor on your specific needs while planning a backpacking trip so you can avoid having an energy crash and potentially placing you and others in your group in danger.

The fact is, on the trail you need calories because they convert to energy. You need some complex and simple carbs and fat and protein and sugar.

Here is a quick little guide for the types of food you can take, but don't let this list be the end of your research. Do an Internet search for "backpacking nutrition," and get ready for a lot of data to consider.

For the quick little three-nighters, you may not need to put a lot of thought into planning your food, but on the month-long treks, I highly recommend it. Check with your doctor for more details on what you may need.

# Fats/Protein

**Beef jerky** – My buddy Josh took along some home-made jerky on one of our trips, and it really tasted good. Since it gave us the right type of nutrition that we needed, it was a bonus. Store-bought jerky will work as well, but don't buy the jerky weeks before your trip, as it may go bad. I bought some and put it in my gear closet for a trip, the trip got canceled, and when I found it, I had a bag filled with green fur-looking stuff.

Anything fatty or with protein is good. You can take some summer sausage or pepperoni, or even some of the dehydrated eggs for breakfast will be good. A lot of the dehydrated meals I take are loaded with protein, so check out the meals as well.

**Trail mix** – A great source of healthy fat, but don't eat too much of it. One source of research I found stated that nuts, which are high in omega-6, can cause constipation, which might actually not be a bad thing on a trip. Mix in some dried fruit and dark chocolate. My trail mix consists of the basic GORP: Good Ol' Raisins and Peanuts. I also add some almonds. I have a bag of dried banana chips in my pack as well.

**Hard cheese** – If the weather is cooler, take some hard block cheese. You can snack on it with a few crackers while you are hiking. Also, with some pita bread, or some tortilla shells, the cheese, along with some summer sausage (again if the weather is a bit cooler) and some spices, might make a nice little pita pizza or taco wrap once warmed by the fire.

# Carbs

**Dehydrated fruits and vegetables** – apples, mangoes, sweet potato chips, bananas, raisins, and the like. These can be found already packaged on the snack aisle of your grocery store, or you may want to consider putting together your favorites and bag them yourself for each day.

**Dates** – are lightweight, starchy, and packed full of carbs.

**Dehydrated potatoes** – are great on the trail. I have used some prepackaged with bacon and three-cheese and herbs. They are ready for you to eat once you add the water and are quite tasty.

Same as counting every ounce when trying to go light, when talking about food, you want to carry as many calories as you can in the forms of fat, proteins, and carbs. One school of thought is to eat junk food while hiking, and eat carbs and protein for dinner. Some summer sausage or pepperoni with some ramen noodles or potatoes will work.

I'm one of those people who can talk to anyone, and one weekend my wife and I went to a neighborhood-wide yard sale, and I started talking to the lady at one place we stopped. The woman mentioned she was a dietitian, so I asked her to tell me in a quick sentence when and what should someone eat while on a week-long backpacking trip.

She told me to carb load at night, and eat protein in the morning for the energy. I used to think eating protein at night was the way to go, and she said it would be okay, but it was crucial to eat some protein a few hours prior starting your activity. You may get several answers from several people you may talk to, so consult with your doctor to get the right game plan.

Some recommend doing a carb-load at night so your body can store the energy and use it the next day while expelling energy on the trail. At night, as your body digests the food while you sleep, your body generates heat, which helps warm you up at night. Then, as you hike, you deplete the stored energy and start to slow down. Eat something sugary to give you the immediate energy you need to make that last mile or two.

Look at the food you like, evaluate the weight, and decide if you want to take it.

Remember that the key here is to take the foods you like to eat and taste good to you—as well as the right kinds of food. I take a ton of snacks for the trail, but a diabetic will probably have different needs from mine.

Food is awesome. We do quite a bit of socializing around food in one way or another. Many churches still have "Dinner on the Ground" (at least that is what we used to call it). That is usually the event where you are able to get to know each other within the congregation. Since you can't actually talk during the service, you may make some plans to go to lunch or maybe dinner with other members.

When dating, couples probably still go for a meal like dinner or lunch. Lunches are great first date meals because if it is going poorly, you both know it will be over in less than an hour—thank goodness for the one-hour first date. Maybe you went for a cup of coffee to get to know each other. At least that is what I did back in my day. Did I just say back in my day? Wow, I must be getting older than I realized.

Bottom line: we love to eat. We have to eat to live so we may as well make the food taste good, right? The trail is no different. Bland food is bad. Do you like to eat bland food at home? Do you want bland food while backpacking? Probably not. For me, the dinner around the campfire is what I look forward to most on a trip. Sure, the scenery and conversation are great, and the jokes and banter along the trail are also great, but I enjoy the dinner around the campfire.

You can get imaginative with your trail meals, just make sure that they are light. I can offer a few tips, but keep in mind, I am not a vegetable guy. I like my meat and potatoes. Planning your food ahead of time will help you know how much food per day you need, as well as how much weight you are taking.

There are many types of backpacking foods out there, and sometimes you can use your imagination. Mountain House has great backpacking food. I have tried several of their meals, but I keep going back to spaghetti and meat sauce in the Pro Pack. The Pro Pack is vacuum-sealed so it is in a smaller package, which means it takes up less space. However, I have a tip on how to make that tight little package even lighter, so keep reading.

I have tried their breakfast meals, but I usually stick to my favorite breakfast choice of Pop-Tarts, coffee, and oatmeal. I have been eating this on the trail for years, and I keep coming back to it. You may find your favorite meal combinations as well.

Don't stop with Mountain House. There are many companies, for example Harmony House, that sell bulk items like vegetables and meat. Well, they call it TVP (meat substitute).

Their meat substitutes are called "Chikenish bits" and "Beefish Bits." I use these with some ramen noodles or to add to my spaghetti for dinner for a little extra protein.

If you do an Internet search for "backpacking food" with the quotes, you will get many links that are related to dehydrated foods, how to dehydrate, and how to make your own lightweight foods. At the time I was writing this section, I got over 223,000 results. While editing this section, months later, I searched again with Google, and I got about 307,000 results. So there is no telling how many more will be there by the time you read this section. Have fun.

The thing to remember is that you need to take light food because this is where much of your pack weight will come from. If you are already taking all dry food like crackers and bread or dehydrated food like ramen noodles, then you are ahead of the game.

I have even tried to dehydrate my own chicken, and although it tasted fine, I didn't like the texture, and it took way too much fuel to rehydrate, so I switched to taking the "Chickenish Bits." I tested these from home first, then on the trail. They are very light, rehydrate quickly, and are quite tasty—just add some pepper or your spice of choice.

Don't limit yourself to online shopping for good backpacking foods. Check out the grocery store next time, look down all the aisles for the light, dry, dehydrated foods, and see what you might like. I have tried the cup-o-noodles as well as the chicken-flavored ramen noodles with some foil-packed chicken to add to the mix. Or the beef flavor with some summer sausage added.

The grocery store can be a great place to start you on the right path to Gram Weenieism if you stay away from anything that contains water.

The main thing to remember here is to take what you like. If you want to take a jar of peanut butter and a couple of pita bread slices, go for it. That might be a tasty breakfast item, and peanut butter has protein.

Remember that we are trying to go light, so think about some tortillas and a few slices from a block of cheese with some pepperoni slices heated in the fire. You can make a nice little pizza wrap. Add some spices, and you could make others in your group jealous.

Instant potatoes with some Chickenish Bits from Harmony House is great. In this mix, you have the carbs and the protein. Anything instant is what you are looking for. Some of the Beefish Bits and a package of roast beef ramen noodles are nice, too. Use your imagination here, and you will be surprised what you can come up with.

Some instant Aunt Jemima pancakes would be great if you could figure out how to cook them without having to lug a skillet and oil around. Hmmmm . . . what could we do here?

Here is what you can do with the pancake mix, but please test it from home first so you don't end up with a mess while backpacking. Get one of your carabiners off your pack or a rock or something small enough to fit into the bottom of your cook pot. Pour enough water into the pot to have about two inches above your rock or 'biner.

Have a premeasured amount of pancake mix and the water needed. You will have to have figured this out ahead of time, based on the instructions on the box.

Add the water (cold and filtered) to the mix in a thick Ziploc freezer bag, and mix it until you have the correct consistency. Put the bag into the boiling water, and let it cook. Just keep an eye on it so it does not overcook, and make sure you keep the plastic away from the flame.

Pull out the bag, and you have a pancake biscuit. Since you are testing from home, and if it tastes good, imagine how it will taste on one of those cold early mornings. Mmmm. When testing meals at home, I have found that they taste ten times better on the trail.

## Snacks

The idea with snacks is to take lightweight food, but food that you enjoy, just like your meals. I have taken the peanut M&Ms, trail mix, Gatorade powder packets, and even crackers with cheese. Not all on the same trip, mind you, this is just a list of things I have taken in the past. Almonds, trail mix, oh wait, I already mentioned trail mix. I take trail mix on every trip because of the calories contained within. Plus the dietary needs are there. Nuts contain fat and protein; the M&Ms have the sugar. Therefore, it is a good food to take, and you might enjoy the taste.

One cup of sliced almonds contain 20 grams of protein. One cup of raisins has 6 grams of protein. There is not much fat in raisins at 0.8 grams, but 1 cup of almonds contains 45 grams of fat. One cup of sliced almonds has 529 calories. Calories are what fuels your body for the trip, so while on the trail, you need calories to be able to make each mile. Junk food has a lot of calories, so this is what you need for snacks. Snack as much as you feel the need while hiking. Once you are at camp, fix some good, hearty meals.

Take some sports drink packets to replace the electrolytes you sweat out and to make the water taste better. People don't drink enough water on the trail, which is bad. Headaches and cramps are just a couple of the symptoms of dehydration. Medicinenet.com has a list of other symptoms of dehydration:

- Dry mouth
- The eyes stop making tears
- Sweating may stop
- Muscle cramps
- Nausea and vomiting
- Heart palpitations
- Lightheadedness (especially when standing)
- Weakness
- Decreased urine output

Remember the rule of three? About three days without water . . .

The key is to take plenty of calories as well as what you enjoy eating. I have eaten my weight in CLIF bars over the years and have gotten to the point where I need a change. They are a great source of calories, which we all need on the trail. Since I like variety in my food bag, I have taken my favorite candy bars in place of the CLIF bars because, well, I just love the Snickers bars. A Snickers bar has 250 calories. I also checked a Butterfinger, and it also has 250 calories. You may turn into a calorie counter when planning your snacks; just make sure to count enough.

Bad-tasting food, or even the wrong type of food, can make for a miserable trip. Do not take high-protein, sugar-packed bars for *all* your meals and snacks. This would be bad.

A tip on how to lighten your load with food is to replace the original packaging. If possible, take your crackers out of the box and put them in a Ziploc bag. For your freeze-dried meals, remove the contents from the original aluminum foil pack and put it all in a freezer bag, making sure to remove the moisture packet. I use a pot cozy made out of Reflectix to help make my plastic bag stand upright. It also keeps the food hot while it rehydrates. You should be able to purchase it at most any building supply store. Mark on the bag how much water to add, and seal it up. This serves a few purposes:

- You can lay the bag flatter so it is less bulky.
- You eat out of the bag so you don't need to take a bowl.
- Since you don't need a bowl, you don't need to take any soap to wash the bowl after you eat.
- You can add your own spices to the Ziploc bag.
- You also have a Ziploc bag to seal up your trash so you can carry it out.

The freezer bag weighs less than the foil pack. Remember, every ounce counts. Some might say, "He's crazy to go through all that." Remember back when I said you will be mocked for some of the stuff you do as a Gram Weenie? This most assuredly brings some comments. Let the math do the talking.

Compare the empty foil pack to a plastic freezer bag. The results are as follows:

Pack of lasagna with meat sauce:
Full foil pack of food = $4\frac{3}{4}$ ounces
Freezer bag of food = $4\frac{1}{4}$ ounces

Therefore, you can see that using the quart size freezer bag saved me $\frac{1}{2}$ ounce for one meal. On a four-night trip with four meals, you save two whole ounces. If you did this with just your evening meals, on a one-week long trip, you could save a lot of weight. Seven evening meals, saving $\frac{1}{2}$ ounce per meal, is a savings of four ounces over taking the aluminum packaging. That is quarter of a pound. Are you starting to see the light yet? If not, keep reading, the light is just around that next tree.

Since every ounce counts, and you have to pack out the trash, the plastic freezer bag is the lighter way to go. One aspect of being a Gram Weenie is to plan the trip ahead of time so you can pack lighter. And packing out your trash needs to be considered here since leaving your trash out there in the middle of the trail is just wrong on many levels. I have found that placing one plastic closable bag into another is easier than placing an aluminum bag into another aluminum bag.

The phrase "pack it in, pack it out" refers to your trash. Don't leave your trash behind for someone else to carry out. You carried it into the woods; you had better be the one who carries it out. We have seen that people have left their trash around on several trips, and it is very annoying. Hikers have enough to worry about without having to carry your garbage out.

As you plan a trip, you need to be aware of how much food you take. This is a very difficult thing to accomplish. Each trip will determine how much food and what types of food you will be taking, so obviously, the weight of your food bag will change from trip to trip.

On some trips, I still end up with an extra candy bar or pack of ramen noodles, but for the most part I am doing better now than I have only a few years earlier. Almost every backpacker that I have talked to has admitted to taking too much food, so you are not alone.

The food you take will taste good to you, and it will taste good to the critters that are out there as well. On the Appalachian Trail, where I generally hike, the shelters are equipped with steel cable and pulley devices for you to hang your food at night. Even though we camp on the Appalachian Trail, we still sleep in our hammocks, but we use the privy and the cable system to hang our food.

It is a good idea to hang your food anytime you will not be in camp. For example, at Stover Creek Shelter, we had a group of about seven or eight, and some of them wanted to take a day hike down to Three Forks to see the sights. Some of them went and some stayed behind. Had we all gone on the day hike, we would have hung our food. We felt safe that if at least one of us stayed behind, the food would have been safe from scavenging critters.

Just because you are diligent with keeping your food out of camp does not mean others are. The critters in the woods know where to find food, and they are used to finding food at these shelters along the trail. They know what a tent looks like and know they will usually find something edible in the tents and the backpacks. I read a story on www.timesleader.com about a scout who had some candy in his tent and was attacked by a bear; ". . . smaller size Snickers bars were found at the scene," the article said. It seems that the bear was attracted to the candy bars and ripped the tent up to get to the sweet treat. The bear grabbed the young scout by the pocket and dragged him off into the woods. Long story short, the kid survived the attack.

On a trip to the Smoky Mountains, there were many of us sleeping in a shelter. The guy who was sleeping next to me asked one morning, "Did that critter mess with you last night?" I asked what critter, and he showed me his toilet paper roll. He said that he kept feeling something crawling around his head and hearing something messing around in his pack, and it kept him up all night. It seems that the critter, we assumed a rat, had gotten into his pack and gorged himself on the toilet paper roll the guy stored in his pack. (It must have been scented toilet paper.)

When we go backpacking, we hang anything with an odor. We hang our food, of course, but we also hang our TP, baby wipes, toothpaste, and even our toothbrushes, , sunscreen, pills, lip balm, anything.

Here is a quick tip: If you have many backpackers in the group, and a lot of food in the group, it is a good idea to use an empty pack to hang your food. Just do *not* seal the bag completely. I met a guy at Wise Shelter in Virginia who told me he had some food in his pack, and he zipped it up tight and hung it in the trees. Some critter not only got to his food, it tore his pack up to get to the treats. Please leave your pack open so if something does manage to get to your food, it won't destroy your pack in the process. Better to lose a few calories than to lose an expensive pack.

On one of the camping trips my father took me on, he slept in a Volkswagen camper/bus and I, along with a friend, slept in a tent. We kept a loaf of bread and other snacks in the tent with us, and at some point during the night, a critter gnawed through the tent, through the bag that held the food, and through the thin plastic that held the loaf of bread. The area where the animal had eaten was a perfectly spherical section from the loaf. It was about the size of a golf ball. We were amazed at how perfectly smooth the section was.

There are quick and easy ways to hang your food if you are in an area that does not provide you with an apparatus you can use. You can throw a rope over a tree branch and pull your bag up at least eight feet or so. Tie off one end to a tree and hope for the best.

## Your Lightweight Fire Kit

I have seen some very elaborate fire kits that folks carry in their packs. To be honest, I have also carried a ton of fire-making implements. I do have a FireSteel and a striker. My striker is an empty disposable lighter that I cut the bottom out of and gutted. It works great with dry tinder in optimum conditions, but I have jute twine packed into the bottom of the lighter in case I need it.

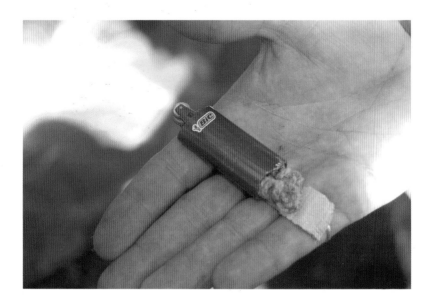

I also follow the "Two means one, one means none" rule when it comes to fire. That means that if I lose the striker or the steel, I have the other one as a backup. I carry a lighter in my pocket on every trip.

Fire is one thing you do not want to be without in the middle of a forest. I have also carried some cotton balls soaked in wax. They are great when you're trying to get a fire going. A stick or knife can break up the cotton ball, a spark from my steel or striker, and you have a flame that will burn for at least ten minutes. Yes, I timed it when I tested it from home.

Now some may say that it is too much. "All you need is one mini disposable lighter" is what I keep hearing from people, but on one trip, we could not get a fire started with a little disposable lighter. Guess who stepped up and saved the day. Yup, that would be me. Three of the guys in our group who were giving me a hard time about some of my backpacking contraptions I had (they called me MacGyver) shut up quickly when I got the fire going with a wax-soaked cotton ball. I was the hero for the night. To be a true practitioner of Gram Weenieism, I should only take one mini disposable lighter, but I don't want to be without fire.

On warmer weather trips, you may only need a little lighter, or a fire steel, but in the winter, like on the trip mentioned above, when the wind is whipping around and there's snow on the ground, you have to be imaginative on how you get a fire going. Even wet wood has dry wood deep underneath the bark, or you can find dry wood hanging in the trees, but you have to look for it. To be on the safe side, you still may need a backup plan for making fire—a second lighter or some wax-soaked cotton.

If the one lighter I have gets lost, wet, or runs out of fuel, I have a backup. Which means I have fire. Which means I have a way to keep warm and boil water to purify or cook with. Be smart with some of these things. Being safe on the trail is very important, and fire can play a huge part. I keep the little hollowed out bic lighter packed with jute twine or dryer lint in my pack, but like I said above, I have a backup lighter in my pocket.

Fire can keep you warm during the cold months as well as ward off the night-time critters, and with fire, you can make questionable water safe to drink. You need to use your head, and safety should be at the forefront of your thoughts long before you make your first footprint at the trail-head.

Bottom line here is that you need to have some sort of dependable fire and know how to make a fire. Are you familiar with the fire triangle?

The US Forest Service says this about fire:

What is Fire?

"Fire is a significant force in the forest environment. Depending upon the specific land management objective and a host of environmental variables, fire will sometimes be an enemy, sometimes a friend, and frequently its effects will be mixed between the two extremes."

Fire Triangle:

In order to have a fire, there must be three elements:

Fuel: something that will burn (such as paper, wood, etc.)

Heat: enough to make the fuel burn

Oxygen: the air we breathe

Remove one of these three elements and the fire will go out.

On the trail, fuel could be the dry leaves on the ground or other natural material, like small twigs and other sticks, and then larger sticks and logs.

Oxygen is a given, so next you need a heat source. Here is where your disposable lighter or fire steel comes into play. A spark from your steel will not ignite a stick, a twig, or even a leaf. You need tiny fibrous materials small enough and with enough surface area to catch the spark you can blow into a flame. We call this a bird's nest.

Making a bird's nest takes practice. This is why I recommend keeping some jute twine, cotton, or dryer lint handy. You can pull out a few pieces and set them in the middle of where your fire will be. Arrange some leaves under the lint and you can direct your spark into the lint.

Start out making your bird's nest with pine needles, leaves, bark, paper, or anything that you can form into a nest, and put a small amount of cotton into the middle. Then use your striker to throw a spark into the cotton, and it usually lights rather quickly. You can then stick the burning nest into your fire structure.

There are several ways to build a fire, but here is the way I usually do it.

Build your fire structure foundation with some larger sticks to block the wind. On top of the foundation, pile on leaves and smaller sticks no larger than a cigar. Stack those sticks into a tepee shape. Some argue that the triangle shape works better than the log cabin shape and vice versa. I don't have a dog in that fight, so I stay out of it, and while they argue this point, I get my fire going and start relaxing.

The trick is to build the fire using very small twigs and gradu-ate up to the larger ones. Log cabin, tepee, or just a pile is not important. Using small pieces of material is.

## Personal Kit

My personal kit changes from trip to trip. On one trip we hiked up the Approach Trail to Springer Mountain. I was still recovering from two surgeries, and I had to take some extra items in the form of medical supplies. Long story short, I had major surgery a few months before the trip, and the week before the trip, the surgeon had to cut me open near my belly button to remove some infection because my body was "rejecting the sutures."

In the end, I had a hole in my stomach, so my personal kit included some latex gloves, gauze pads, and a bottle of clean ster-ile water. Every morning and evening, I had to pull gauze out of the hole, replace it with clean gauze, and patch the hole with fresh gauze and tape. I love hiking so much that I was not going to let a hole in my stomach keep me from the trail.

Usually, my personal kit includes a roll of TP, pain pills, Handi Wipes, and some maintenance meds that I have to take. I also have deodorant (depending on the time of year), my toothbrush, which I cut in half to shave some weight, and toothpaste pods. I take these pods in lieu of taking a tube of toothpaste. The ones shown here are ready to go and scaled out at 3/8 of an ounce. For scale, here they are next to a full-size toothbrush.

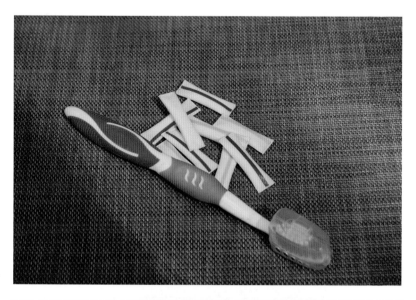

My personal kit consists of my personal stuff as well as my first-aid kit, which is limited. Having a limited first-aid kit is a personal choice, and you may find that in a group of five hikers, you will find five very different first-aid and personal kits. These two kits are the areas where you and only you can make the decision on what to take. Don't let anyone talk you out of or into taking greater or fewer items than you believe you will need.

I have seen some first-aid kits that would rival a first responder's kit, although while thru-hiking, an elaborate kit might be ideal. But for our little weeklong trips, which we usually take in larger groups, an abridged version meets our needs.

If you ask fifteen backpackers what is in their first-aid kit, you might get twenty answers, as some may have multiple kits (one for each season they hike). Put together your own kit based on your skill level with self-rescue techniques and ability to function under pressure.

In your personal kit, you will want the obvious things, like TP, cleansing products, toothpaste, medications, deodorant, and anything else you need on a daily basis for your personal hygiene.

## Cook Kit

Again, we're at a crossroads.

"When you come to a fork in the road, take it." —Yogi Berra

This is again a time for you to dig deep and decide: stove or no stove. Some hardcore ultra-light campers may opt to use their campfire to cook their dinner or boil their water for the dehydrated meals. For me, I have opted for the DIY stove from time to time. Here is one that is easy to make. It is a bean dip can, I think. All you need is some sort of solid fuel and a way to keep the pot elevated above the flame a bit.

The easiest way is to make the stove from a cat food can. Search online for instructions if you want to go the route of a DIY soda can stove.

On the colder trips, however, you might regret it. The fuel needs to be kept warm, and if you forget to keep it warm at night, like in your sleeping bag, it prolongs "coffee o'clock" and breakfast.

On a trip in March, a very cold March, I had a DIY stove made from an aluminum bottle. It worked great and boiled my water quickly, but I had to keep the fuel, which was denatured alcohol, protected from the harsh cold air. I forgot about the fuel and left it in my bag exposed to the cold environment.

The fuel would not light. I placed the fuel bottle in my coat and had to walk around the camp waiting for it to warm up. Once it was warm, I cranked it up and made coffee. The fuel for these DIY stoves usually has to be protected from the cold air so they are more efficient while burning. It would had taken more fuel to get my coffee going, which may have been an issue later on in the trip if I had not planned on taking enough fuel.

I have gone back to my Soto Micro regulator stove and a canister of compressed gas. It is more dependable than the DIY stoves in my opinion. Not as light, mind you, but more dependable.

There are several types of stoves out there. Stoves run off liquid fuel, compressed gas, and then the DIY stoves that run off isopropyl and denatured alcohol. The DIY stoves also run off HEET.

Many thru-hikers who I have met prefer the DIY stoves because they are light and easy to make. Since they run off HEET and denatured alcohol, the fuel is easy to purchase throughout the towns on the long-distance trails. The denatured alcohol is also easy to find in the stores along the trail.

Since you can't mail fuel, long-distance hikers have to replace their fuel as they go, so I can understand the logic behind the DIY stoves. They are easy to make, and the fuel is easy to purchase while on the trail (should you find a store). However, for a weekend or even a one-week-long trip, I prefer my micro regulator stove and fuel canister. On my next trip, I am considering boiling my water next to the fire to avoid the weight of stoves and fuel.

Another option is a dual-walled wood-burning stove. Again, this one is a DIY stove and can be made from a one-quart paint can and a few other materials. You can paint it with a high-temperature flat black paint to help with the protection from the elements as well as to help hold the heat. This is a great stove.

As the wood burns, the gas comes up in between the walls and reignites, and this is where you get the heat to boil your water. I have tested this once on a trip to see if it worked, and it worked great. This type of stove is light, easy to make, and has an unlimited source of fuel, as long as you are in a wooded area, and it is not raining. But who wants to process wood in the morning? It only prolongs my getting coffee, which is a priority to me.

You have to make these DIY stoves, and as a DIY'er myself, I love to make and alter my gear. However, depending on your trip, you may need something more dependable. Some may argue that a DIY soda can stove is the most dependable. I find it difficult to agree with this. I have used my SOTO on so many trips, and I take care of it, so for me, this is a very dependable stove.

# CHAPTER SEVEN

# WATER TREATMENT

The human body is made up of around 60 percent water. Water is essential to body functionality and ultimately our survival. This is why having clean, drinkable water is also crucial on the trail.

The lightest possible way to make water "safe to drink" is to boil it. Period. I say the lightest because you don't need to take any filtration device with you. All you need to do is gather water in a metal container, boil it, and after a few minutes, all the little critters swimming around in there will be dead. It is now safe to drink.

It may be safe to drink, but not "drinkable," in my opinion.

Dirty, brown, nasty water that has been boiled is now "safe to drink." However, who wants to drink a glass of water that you scooped out of a pond?

Not me. Unless, of course, you are in a survival situation, in which case you may not even want to boil it and take the chance and drink it anyway. But when backpacking, we have the ability to filter the water or some other way to rid our water of all the water-borne pathogens so we don't get sick when we drink from water sources. These little critters can be in any body of water out there, so be careful.

When backpacking, we usually are near some sort of stream that has clear water running along, but I still want to be on the side of caution instead of being reckless. I boiled water that came from a river or a stream, but this is to save my filter. If you only have a puddle or a pond and a dirty water source, you may as well filter it if you have a filter.

For me, "drinkable" water is colorless, tasteless, and odorless. I take a filter.

The lightest way is to boil it, but the next lightest option is to take the chemicals—either drops or pills.

If you want to go ultra-light, fine. This is a personal journey, so feel free to take the chemicals. However, you do have other options. Once you have been on a trip with a filter, you may find that the filtered water is more enjoyable to drink than chemically-treated water or even dirty water that has been filtered through a bandana and then boiled or treated.

Water treatment options are plentiful. However, you may see several basic types of filters on the market these days. The Steri-Pen is a device that uses ultraviolet light to kill the microbial critters. There are also pump, chemical, and gravity filters.

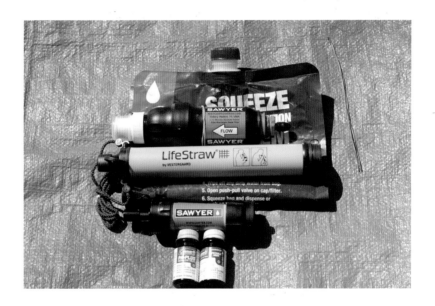

Here is my MSR filter, the Swetwater filter. This is a great pump filter that I have taken on many trips.

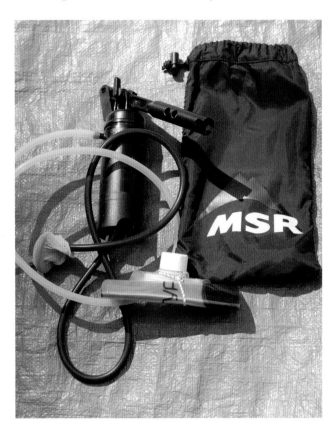

Katadyn also makes a great filter. I have not owned one, but I have been on a few trips where one of the members of my group had one and he loved it. Some filters are pump and some are gravity. All are great filters, and some weigh less than others, so research what options you have in your area, and select the one that you think will be best for your needs.

I opt for the Sawyer filter, which will filter the water down to 0.10 absolute microns. That is not only a filter to remove any solids but also enough to filter out the smallest of microbial critters that would cause issues on the trail. The result is some great-tasting water. Oh yeah, the filter and one plastic bag (included in the purchase) weighs in at three ounces.

What can be said for water treatment? Which is more important to you, safe-to-drink water, drinkable water, or clean, colorless, and tasteless filtered water?

I have talked with some thru-hikers up on the AT, and a few use the water treatment pills for their entire trip. The whole 2200-ish miles. Not me. I do not like the idea of drinking chemicals, if I can avoid it. This is why I go backpacking . . . to get away from all the chemicals in the air and water, not put more into my system.

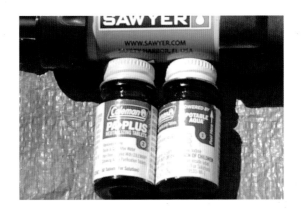

Sure, in a survival situation, I can understand using the pills. I even have some of these pills on hand in my get home bag should I find myself in some sort of apocalypse while on the road. But I prefer to filter out my bugs, not kill them with drugs. DOH! Did that just rhyme? I totally did not mean to do that.

First, we need to understand what can cause the water to be bad for us to drink while out on the trail. In some of the standing bodies of water, you have to worry about the sediment that can accumulate throughout the water. Algae, tiny bugs, silt, and so forth. Depending on the individual environment, the sediment may not be bad to drink, but why chance it?

These items can be filtered out with your bandana. Wrap the bandana around the opening of your water bottle and submerge the bottle to gather the water. You still may find that the water is a color other than clear, but at least the water will not have any or very little sediment and larger particles.

Then you have the really bad stuff—the living critters. Cryptosporidium and Giardia are the microscopic, water-borne pathogens found in natural bodies of water. Yes, even the fast moving streams and rivers. And yes, even the rolling areas where the water is rolling over rocks in the middle of the rapids of a river. Cryptosporidium and Giardia do not care if the water is moving or still, so don't be foolish and trust it.

You may get lucky or you may end up with a bad bellyache ruining your trip and endangering your health at the same time. I talked with a guy at REI who has thru-hiked the AT a couple of times. He told me that he was way high up in the mountains, away from civilization, and he took a drink from a stream coming off of the mountains. It was melted snow . . . and he got sick. He didn't filter it. He said that now, he filters every drop of water he drinks, regardless of his altitude in the mountains. He had to find help quick, and he was out for a couple of weeks recovering. It can be pretty bad, so do you really want to chance it?

## Cryptosporidium and Giardia

This is from Wikipedia.com:

"Cryptosporidium is a genus of apicomplexan protozoans that can cause gastrointestinal illness with diarrhea in humans. Cryptosporidium is the organism most commonly isolated in HIV-positive patients presenting with diarrhea. Treatment is symptomatic, with fluid rehydration, electrolyte correction and management of any pain. Cryptosporidium oocysts are 4-6 μm in diameter and exhibit partial acid-fast staining. They must be differentiated from other partially acid-fast organisms."

From Medicinenet.com:
What are the symptoms of cryptosporidiosis?

• Stomach cramps or pain
• Dehydration

- Nausea
- Vomiting
- Fever
- Weight loss

"Giardia is a genus of anaerobic flagellated protozoan parasites of the phylum Sarcomastigophora that colonise and reproduce in the small intestines of several vertebrates, causing giardiasis. Their life cycle alternates between an actively swimming trophozoite and an infective, resistant cyst. Giardia were first described by the Dutch microscopist Antonie van Leeuwenhoek in 1681.1 The genus is named after French zoologist Alfred Mathieu Giard."[2]

What are the symptoms of giardiasis?

- Diarrhea
- Abdominal pain
- Cramping
- Bloating
- Nausea with or without vomiting
- Malaise, and fatigue
- Fever is unusual

"The severity of the symptoms may vary greatly from mild or no symptoms to severe symptoms. Stools may be foul smelling when the Giardia interferes with the absorption of fat from the intestine (malabsorption). The illness or the malabsorption may cause loss of weight."

"Symptoms and signs of giardiasis do not begin for at least seven days following infection, but can occur as long as three or more weeks later. In most patients the illness is self-limiting and lasts 2–4 weeks. In many patients who are not treated, however, infection can last for several months to years with continuing symptoms. Children with chronic infection may fail to thrive. Some patients recover from their giardiasis, with or without treatment, but symptoms continue, perhaps because of a condition referred to as post-infectious irritable bowel syndrome. The cause of the continuing symptoms is not clear but may be due to bacterial overgrowth of the small intestine."

These are unicellular parasites about three to five microns in diameter. Unfortunately, according to some of my research on this matter, Cryptosporidium is supposed to be resistant to chlorine disinfection. Other research says yes and some no to the question, "Can I treat my water with bleach?" Therefore, the theory of treating your liter of water with four drops of common household bleach might be a gamble—one that I am not willing to take.

This is why I like to take my Sawyer filter.

I have taken the Sawyer squeeze filter on many trips and love it. Like I said, the filter and one 2.5 liter water bag weighs three ounces. That is my water kit. Three ounces. And the Sawyer is good for a million gallons. That's right. One million—if you take care of the filter.

The filter even comes with a large syringe to help you wash it after each trip, so take really good care of it.

Do the math on one million gallons.

Let's say that you will use this filter in your day-to-day life and not while backpacking.

You drink five gallons of water a day.

Three hundred sixty-five days in a year, times 5 gallons a day is 1,825 gallons a year.

One million gallons divided by 1,825 is 547.945 years.

Wow. Imagine how long it will last if you only took it backpacking a few times a year. It will literally be the last filter you may ever buy. Don't take chances on the water you drink, filter it.

# CHAPTER EIGHT

# CLOTHES

When we discussed protection from the elements in Chapter Three, we focused on the shelter when you are asleep. Proper protection from the elements, when hiking or simply hanging out at the campsite, is just as important. When it comes to staying warm with the clothes on your back, you need to be aware of the different types of fabric that are out there.

Two terms are very important when protecting yourself from the elements while backpacking: hypothermia and hyperthermia.

Hypothermia is when your core temperature drops below 35.0°C (95.0°F), the temperature for normal metabolism and body function.

Hyperthermia is when the body takes in more heat than it releases.

You can see that regulating your body's core temperature is very important while backpacking. You can't just say you're too cold and run inside to get warm. You need to know how to regulate your temperature with the clothes you have so you don't get too warm or too cold. Getting too warm is also a concern because you may begin to sweat profusely.

To regulate your body's temperature, you need to adjust the layers you are wearing. But what type of clothing should you get?

The bottom line is this: Stay away from cotton when backpacking, especially in the cooler months. The phrase we use is Cotton Kills, and here is why: Cotton holds water more than your synthetic materials such as polyester and nylon. So when cotton is wet, it loses its insulating value, unlike wool, which will retain its insulating value even when wet. So if you must wear natural material, give wool a shot.

When water evaporates, the surface that holds the water cools down. So if you have on cotton while hiking, and you get wet, you will need to dry that article of clothing as soon as possible. Your clothes protect you from the elements, so if you are in wet clothes, you will cool off faster and could slip into hypothermia.

Normal human body temperature in adults is 34.4–37.8°C (94–100°F).

Sometimes a narrower range is stated, such as 36.5–37.5°C (98–100°F).

Hypothermia is defined as any body temperature below 35.0°C (95.0°F).

Hypothermia is subdivided into four different levels:

- Mild: 90–95°F (32–35°C)
- Moderate: 82–90°F (28–32°C)
- Severe: 68–82°F (20–28°C)
- Profound: less than 68°F (20°C)

Therefore, you can see that if you wear cotton, you will be colder. Not only when, or if, you fall into the creek and get wet, but when you sweat while hiking, working at camp, gathering wood, and so on. Your best bet is to wear synthetic material.

You will not find any cotton in my pack other than a few bandanas. I stick to the synthetics unless it is my down vest, coat, and sleeping bag.

On the other hand, while hiking in the warmer months, wearing a cotton shirt may prove to be a good idea since you can wet the shirt, put it on, and it will be like standing in front of an air conditioner vent.

We were camping in June one time, and I was so hot I soaked one of my polyester shirts in the creek, wrung out the excess water, and put it on. The relief was wonderful. I cooled down almost instantly—or at least it seemed that way at the time. A cotton shirt would have held the water and kept me cooler longer, but it may not have dried out in time before nightfall, and I could have been in trouble. The thing with cotton is that it takes a while to dry in less than optimal conditions.

In the bright sun, laid out on a rock or hanging on a fence post, sure it may have dried faster. But we were in the woods, in the shade, with a light breeze blowing, so the cotton shirt would have taken too long to dry.

Let's look at the four ways we lose body heat:

- Convection
- Evaporation
- Conduction
- Radiation

## Convection

The most common form of heat loss with clothing is convection. This happens when air (or water) touches and moves away from the skin carrying heat with it. This type of heat loss accounts for the highest percentage of the body's heat loss under normal conditions.

## Evaporation

When you sweat, you produce moisture on your skin. When your sweat evaporates, the moisture turns into vapor. When this happens, the vapor removes heat from your body.

## Conduction

This type of heat loss only has a minor effect. In conductive heat loss, heat is passed directly through a stationary medium that has a lower temperature.

## Radiation

This type of heat loss only occurs to solid objects (like your body). The sun heats up your body through radiation. It doesn't heat up the air directly.

Radiant heat loss from the human body is only minor except when all other channels of heat loss are covered. In hiking situations, radiant heat occurs not from the skin but from the fabric close to the skin.

Heat loss through this channel is prevented or reduced by reflective materials that turn the heat back to the body. This is not always ideal in a hiking situation.

## Layers

Now, let's talk layers: The only thing to remember about staying warm is to not get cold. Now before you say out loud "Duuh, that's obvious," let me explain.

Per the data above, you can slip into dangerous areas if you lose only a few degrees of warmth. Once you get so cold your body starts to shiver uncontrollably, you may have slipped too far to the other side. Once you get to the point when you can't stop shivering, getting warm again might just prove to be a real challenge. To avoid this scenario, you will want to regulate your body's core temperature with layers. Think of it like a thermostat in your home.

As stated before, I ran into this at Ice Water Spring shelter in the Smoky Mountains. I unzipped my bag too fast, and the cold air hit me hard. I could not stop shaking while answering nature's call, and I knew I was in trouble. But luckily for me, and those around me, I was able to increase my temperature and pull out of the danger area.

If you slip into hypothermia, it is not only bad for you but for the rest of your group as well. If you get into this kind of trouble, the burden falls on other folks in your group to get you warm, or to safety, whichever the situation calls for.

This scenario is easily avoidable if you can figure out how to manage your core temperature using the clothes on your back and the clothes you carry with you.

Using layers is how you are able to control your body's core temperature and not get too cold or too warm. There are three primary layers to know about:

- Base Layer
- Insulation Layer
- Shell Layer

## Base Layer

Your base layer needs to have a level of insulation factor. For me, my top base layer is a Patagonia shirt, and it is almost too hot to wear while I am hiking. But at night, oh man, I love it. My bottom layer is REI brand and keeps me just as warm. Both are made from synthetic material. This is also crucial, so pay attention. The base layer needs to have a wicking property as well.

"Wicking" is the process whereby the fabric pulls moisture away from your skin allowing it to evaporate without affecting the temperature of your body and not allowing you to get cold due to the evaporation process. You still don't want to depend on the base layer to remove all the sweat you produce because there are limits to everything. Once you understand all three of the basics, we will go over some scenarios where different applications of different layers will need to be understood.

## Insulation Layer

This layer is just what it sounds like—to insulate you from the cold. It can be fleece, down, polyester, nylon, but never cotton. Cotton kills.

You may need multiple layers based on the weather conditions. If the temperature only drops to 30°F (–1.1°C), you may survive with only one layer of insulation. If the temperature is due to drop down to well below 0°F (–17.8°C), you may need to have multiple layers of insulation or even a layer of down. This is all up to you and your needs. In Georgia, where I do most of my backpacking, the coldest temperature I have been in was 5°F (–15°C), so I can limit my number of insulation layers.

Maybe I should also mention that I am the human furnace. My wife really loves me in the winter time. I actually start out on her side of the bed to warm it up for her, and it only takes me about five minutes. When she climbs in, her side is already warmed up, and she tells me that I am better than an electric blanket.

Some of the guys in the group were still cold in multiple layers, but I had on my base layer, one layer of insulation, and a down jacket, and all that while in my down sleeping bag, I was hot and had to strip down some of those layers. I also have the insulation of my underquilt under my hammock while I am sleeping.

## Shell Layer

The shell is a layer to protect you from the water and wind. When shopping for a shell, remember to keep it light, folks. After all you will be carrying this layer with you unless it is raining while on the trail. I don't mind hiking in the rain, but I won't start out in the rain, if I can avoid it. My shell is a light and thin raincoat with a hood and works great for me.

Your shell can be used in place of an insulation layer, if the weather is too warm for your actual insulation layer but too cold to walk around in just your base layer. The shell is also good for adding extra insulation on top of all your other layers when the temperature drops below the expected. Keeping the wind off of you will prevent one of the four ways of losing heat: convection.

Using your shell to help keep you warm is an option, so keep that in mind when purchasing it. I have worn my raincoat to keep me warm more often than to stay dry. For example, on one trip, I was too warm with my fleece on, so I stripped down to my top base layer and a shirt. I then got a little cold, so I added my shell, and I warmed up quite nicely.

Like with any other gear you have, make sure the gear you select is in working order. Test your base layer while at home by going outside for a while to see how your body reacts to just the base layer. Then add a layer of fleece or just your shell. Learn how your body reacts to each of the layers you will carry so you will know how it reacts on the trail. Test everything.

# CHAPTER NINE

# TEST FROM HOME

Whichever pack you choose, your choice of clothing, water purification methods, or even food choices, you must, and I can't stress this enough, test from home. Test the gear. Wear the clothes. Carry the pack. Then test, wear, and carry it all again. And again. Even if it is something as simple as a disposable lighter you picked up at the gas station on your way to the trail. I can't think of any time when I bought a lighter, even if it was in a package, that I didn't test before or immediately after I bought it. Make sure you can make fire with the thing because if you don't test it, and you get out on the trail and it doesn't work, you have no one to blame but yourself.

I once found myself in a predicament with a DIY rain fly. Had I tested it from home under more rigorous conditions, I would have found the flaw earlier, and I would not have suffered as much on the trail. I made a rain fly out of some Tyvek material, and not five minutes into setting it up, in the dark no less, one of the tie-outs ripped along the area where I sewed in the loop.

On one trip, I had grabbed a lighter off the dresser on my way out the door because I did not remember packing one. At the campsite, I tried to use it and it failed. I had grabbed an empty lighter. Lucky for me I actually did pack a lighter in my cook kit, so I was okay. Had I not, I would have been up the creek and cold if none of the other hikers had a lighter either.

I have even run into a self-proclaimed "expert" at Black Gap shelter on the Approach Trail. She was starting a thru-hike, and she didn't even know how to use her DIY soda can stove. She stated that a friend gave it to her, but she had never tested it. This is a bad idea, in my opinion. Always, always, always test from home so you know how to use the gear.

I had to show her how to light and how to extinguish the flame. When she asked me if I knew what kind of fuel to burn with the stove, I almost fainted. "You are thru-hiking?" I asked as I sat down to keep from falling.

She would have been out of luck had there not been anyone to show her how to use it. I'm sure she would have eventually learned how to operate it, but she would have been more confident on the trail if she had tested from home.

There are some things I think all hikers should have on them at all times. I don't care if there are twenty folks in your group. All hikers should have, at the very least, the five Cs. Let's say you get separated from the group and are lost. Can you make fire for warmth, protection, and to boil questionable water? Even if you can make fire with a fire bow, you still need to have a disposable lighter or a fire steel handy just in case. You don't want to chance not having a fire.

My bootlaces are not regular laces. They are made of some strong cordage (550 paracord) that can, if needed, double as the string for a fire bow. If I am ever in a "survival situation," I will be able to make fire using primitive techniques.

If you have all the items listed in the Five Cs, test each one of them from home. Can you successfully set up your "Cover" to protect yourself from the elements? Is your knife sharp, and do you really know how to use it? Is your water container good enough to place onto a bed of hot coals to boil water? Is your cordage long enough to use many times—even if you have to cut a length from it?

Test your food. Cook some of the dehydrated foods out there and taste them and maybe even add some of your own spices. Play with the packaging to see if you can make it lighter. Work with your bag as many times as it takes you to pack your items in the best way possible and pack them the same way each trip.

If you cut your toothbrush in half like I discussed earlier, make sure you don't cut it so short that you can't use it. Make sure you can use it with some sort of efficiency so you don't get into any trouble with your dentist.

I can't state this strong enough, but *everything* you have in your pack needs to be tested and used at home before you hit the trail. I even took a nap for a couple of hours in each of my hammocks after I made or bought them. My wife thinks I am crazy, having done some of the things I have done, but I religiously test everything in my pack before it goes on a trip with me. It's better to be safe than sorry. Test how all your gear goes into your pack. Being organized on the trail is as important as it is at home.

# CHAPTER TEN

# ORGANIZATION

When planning for a trip, you may find that organization will fall into place while you get your gear ready. You may want to keep your consumables separate when planning a trip. I plan and organize all of my gear and all of my consumables minus my food when getting ready for a trip. I look at the weather forecast for clothes and cover. I look at the area for certain gear and so on, but I usually put all my food together near the end of my process. This will help you in a few ways:

- You will see your base weight in a pile.
- You will see your consumables separately.
- You will be able to plan more accurately.
- You will be able to weigh each item.
- You will weigh them separately and as a group.

Planning starts way before the actual trip, and if you can separate the groups as you plan, you may just be ahead of the game. Keeping your consumables separate will help you keep a close eye on your fuel, meals, personal items, and snacks. I can't tell you how many trips I have been on where I ran out of my meals and had way too many snacks left over at the end of the trip.

Organization is a crucial part of the Gram Weenie philosophy. How can you know what you have if you don't know where it is? If you don't know where all your gear is and can't get to it when you want to pack for a trip, you may miss out on something. At the very least you may struggle, trying to find that one item, or forget it all together. We were on one trip, and one of my fellow backpackers, who will remain nameless, forgot one of his tree straps for his hammock. DOH! Lucky for him, I had an extra. But those days are gone. I no longer carry anything I don't need. We may have been able to get by with some paracord, but the straps are what you really need with a hammock. I recommend you have two food bags. A larger one that holds *all* your food: dinners and snacks. Keep a smaller bag that holds your snacks for the day you are hiking.

Keep the small bag inside of the larger bag near the top of the backpack. Or store the smaller bag with a daily supply of snacks that goes into one of the side pouches of the pack. It is easy to get to and saves time while you are resting. In the morning, I grab the snacks for the day and place them into the smaller bag. I then place the bag into a side pocket of my pack. As we hike, I can get to the snacks quickly, and at the end of the day, I put the smaller bag into the larger bag until the next morning.

I learned this valuable lesson on the Approach Trail. On one trip, we stopped for a rest, and I took way too long getting some snacks from my pack, which meant less time on my butt resting. It was then that I learned to pack a few snacks into the side pockets of my pack, so the next time we stopped, I grabbed a candy bar and was eating within a few seconds instead of minutes.

For me, the key to a "successful" trip is in what you are willing to learn on that trip. Pay attention to what you are doing when looking for gear. How long did it take to get the item you are looking for? How organized was your pack on the trail?

Designate an area in your house where you can organize your camping gear. If you have a closet, that's great, but even if you have your gear in a chest of drawers, get organized. In a plastic tub, use several tubs with smaller boxes inside. Build some shelves and use tubs, dividers, or whatever you need to do to get organized.

You need to decide how to, what to, and where to organize your gear, but organize in such a way so you know where your hammocks, bug nets, underquilt, and the rest of your gear is located so you can grab each item quickly when planning for a trip.

Regardless of the way you decide to organize, and it may take a few trials to get it the way you want it, keep it that way. Pick a space and set it up. Designate the space as your Gear Closet. Tell the rest of your family that this is your area and to stay out. Well, do this only if you want to be ostracized in your own home. Just keep this area as organized as you can.

However, don't let your organizational skills stop in the closet. Let technology assist you. Use Excel to help you out. All you need to do is get a digital scale so you can weigh each item. Each item should weigh less than twenty pounds, so if your scale is limited to around twenty pounds you should be okay.

To weigh your pack, and the other larger items, get a box, place it on the scale, and zero the scale out. This way, you can set the larger items, like your pack and sleeping bag, into the box and get an accurate weight of each item.

What you do is, weigh the items in ounces, and using the spreadsheet, enter in the weight, and the spreadsheet will convert the item into pounds automatically.

Let the Excel file help you keep your gear organized into a few categories: consumables, sleeping gear, shelter gear, the pack, clothes to be carried, and food. If you are good with Excel, set it up so you enter in the weight of each item, and the sheet does the rest.

## Count the Ounces

Every ounce counts. Another aspect of understanding what a Gram Weenie is may already be apparent to you. I have mentioned counting ounces several times already but have not gotten into the "why" of counting.

You will periodically find something new or something lighter than what you have or something new that will make your trip easier. Every ounce does count, but you need to know the ounces so you can count them.

The three biggest items you will have are your pack, your sleep system, and your shelter. We discussed these earlier, but the following philosophy stands for those three as well.

Weigh everything. Your toothbrush, the rain fly stakes, the TP, as well as the extra batteries you take for your headlamp. Basically you will learn the weight of every item in your pack—or you will be able to look it up if you write it all down. As you weigh each item, look at it and see if you can cut some weight from the items in some way.

More often than not, I hear many folks use the phrase "It doesn't weigh anything" when talking about an item in their pack that they really don't need. This is ridiculous. I just laugh to myself, because everything weighs something.

Even a drop of water weighs something. It may not be measurable on the scales you use, but I will be willing to bet that NASA can tell us how much a drop of water weighs. One site I found states that a drop of water weighs "about .003 ounces." But of course, this all is dependent on the size of the dropper used to make the drop of water.

My research shows me a couple of things. Depending on the size of the dropper used, the weight will differ. Look it up to find out for yourself. The weight of some items may be negligible, but the weight is still there. Basic science tells us that everything that is solid has mass, takes up space, and weighs something.

As you weigh the items in your pack, look at each one. Can you use it as a dual-purpose item or cut the weight down somehow, even by only a few ounces?

Remember this from earlier? One pound of weight equals sixteen ounces. If you can cut just four ounces from four different items in your pack, you just cut sixteen ounces from your pack. Boo-ya, you are now one pound lighter. Who's the Gram Weenie now? That's right, you.

You are on your way.

Part of the organization of your gear is knowing where your gear is located in your closet, but you also need to know how much each item weighs.

## Your Pack

The last area for being organized while you are on the trail is your pack. The more organized your pack is, the more efficiently you will function on the trail.

Knowing where everything is located within your pack is crucial for meeting any challenge that presents itself. What if you are walking along and enjoying the fantastic weather, and the dark clouds roll in and the rain starts to fall?

Quick, where is your rain fly located?

What if you are walking along and get hungry?

Quick, where is your snack bag?

Get the idea? At any point during your trip, you need to know where all your gear is so you can put your hands on it when you need it.

Being organized will let you operate easier on the trail, which will also allow you to enjoy the trip much more.

At the end of a day of hiking, I know where everything is in my pack as I unpack for the night. I have already mentioned my routine when we reach the camping area. I grab my Crocs, rain fly, food, hammock, and so on. This is my routine because I know where all the items are. I have managed to find what works for me, and I keep certain gear in the same spot, either within the pack or strapped to the outside of the pack, on every trip. This is how keeping a good organizational system will pay off. You are organized at home, while planning for a trip, and you are organized on the trail, making your trip more enjoyable.

# CHAPTER ELEVEN

# DUAL-PURPOSE ITEMS

One of the steps in planning right so you can pack light is concentrating on dual-purpose items. This is a hard step to take because it will force you to examine your pack and plan your trips a bit differently than you might be used to. Look at your gear that you plan on putting into that pack, the clothes on your back, and the items in your pockets. Yes, you can even look into your pockets to see if you can cut weight. Let's look at a few items that might be found in a backpack.

Here are just a few ideas on how to limit your weight by selecting dual-purpose items. If you take a large, thick trash bag, you can use this as a rain poncho so you don't need to take a separate one.

Use a tent stake to dig out a fire pit.

Duct tape can be used in first-aid situations or gear and pack repair. Take a medium fixed knife instead of two knives. Socks can be used as a glasses case, pot holder, gloves.

Bandanas can be used to filter water, as a signaling device (if the color is right), or even as a bandage. Trekking poles can be used as a fishing pole or tarp stand. Boot laces, if made of the right material (550 cord), can be used in an emergency to repair gear or even in a fire bow to start a fire.

There are many things you can do with 550 paracord that could go into its own book. There are several inner strands that can be used individually, or as a whole used to secure objects, set snares, repair gear, affix a broken arm into a splint, and so much more.

A coffee cup can be used as a measuring device if it has the markings. The aluminum foil can be used to block the wind from the fire of your stove while you cook but can also be used as a signaling device.

You could take an aluminum water bottle, which is much heavier than your standard Nalgene bottle. The aluminum bottle could replace your cooking pot, if all you plan on doing for dinner is boiling water for your dehydrated food. Compare one aluminum bottle to your drinking bottle plus your cooking pot before making this decision, and count the ounces.

Here you can see my canteen cup by the fire boiling water.

I don't "cook" on the trail anymore; I simply boil water and rehydrate my dinner in freezer bags so there is less cleanup at the end of the meal.

## From Your Pockets

Take only the most important keys you can think of. I take my truck key (if I am the one doing the driving) and my house key if needed. That is all. Once we get to the trailhead, those two keys are wrapped up into a bandana and stored somewhere in my pack.

To lighten my wallet I have a small pocket wallet with only my driver's license, health insurance card, one credit card, and some cash. I take the bare minimum. I don't need pictures, business cards, more than one credit card, yadda yadda yadda. . . . All I need is proof that I can drive, proof I have insurance, some cash for snacks, and stuff before and after, and one credit card for emergencies. I have my folding knife that goes everywhere I go and a lighter. That is all. Nothing more.

Hopefully you will be able to take what you have learned here and apply it to your pack and be able to go a little bit lighter, and be able to look at your pack and the gear within with a fresh perspective. Some might say we are a strange breed because of how we look at things, but the normal is as follows:

"Go ahead and pack it, it doesn't weigh *that* much. . . . It weighs hardly anything. . . . You never know, you might need it. . . ."

We, the practitioners of Gram Weenieism, have trained our brains to think differently about our pack. We are the iconoclasts of the backpacking world. Our normal is this:

"It won't take me long to cut the tags out of this shirt. . . . Ha, I cut my toothbrush in half and shaved three ounces from my pack. . . . I just culled one pair of socks, my Michael Connelly novel, that extra flashlight, and . . . and . . . I cut out half my toilet paper and I shaved a whole pound from my pack!"

Okay first of all, even though I am a firm believer in Gram Weenieism, there are some things I believe you should not skimp on. Toilet paper is one of these things. I have tried to gauge how many sheets I would need for a trip—no I didn't count the sheets, I simply count the bundles I think I might need. However, those trips didn't work out the way I planned, so now I take at least one half of a roll. No more skimping equals no more unpleasant trips. Plus, if I find that I am using less than expected, I have some nice dry tinder for fire making: dual purpose.

Bottom line here is to look at your items and see if you can use them for more than they were designed for. Now, you may not be able to find a dual purpose for every item in your pack, but if you can find more than one purpose for just a couple of items, then you are doing better than most.

# CHAPTER TWELVE

# DIY ITEMS

Another area to lighten your pack might be to make your own gear. It has been my experience that some DIY gear may not cost less money; in fact, most DIY projects, that I have played around with, did cost a bit more. The thing with making your own gear is that you will have the pride of having made it yourself, to your specifications, and it may even be a little bit lighter. Our goal is, after all, obtaining a lighter pack.

Some DIY items I have made are a stove, hammock, rain fly, and even a bug net. I found some wedding tulle, left over from our wedding, and took a large piece of the material and attached the bug net into a DIY hammock I made. It worked great the first night, but on the second night it ripped and was ruined. Luckily, it was a cool night, so bugs were not an issue, but I learned then, on the trip, that tulle is not a good material for bug netting. Had I done a better job testing from home, I would have opted for some other stronger material.

I made a DIY wood saw that I have taken on a few trips. It is fairly light at 9 ⅝ ounces.

I have even made a compact fishing kit with line, weights, and lures out of PVC pipe. It doesn't go backpacking with me because of the weight factor, not to mention I don't want to deal with cleaning and cooking fish. It is primarily for my Get Home Bag. The point is that I made it, and it works—at least in testing it did. I will take it to the pond nearby and really test it, but that is what this is all about. Making something yourself and testing it from home.

I have also modified much of my gear. My ENO hammock, for instance, does not come with a structural ridgeline, so I added one.

My ENO bug net has a zipper that is vertical. In my opinion this is a bad design because to enter a hammock you lay flat and bring your legs into the hammock body. You don't walk upright into the hammock. So I cut the zipper out completely and added some shock cord in the bottom. It works great, and I lightened the load by removing some of the material of the netting as well as the zipper. I did weigh it before and after, and the results are as follows:

Before: 16.72 ounces (474 grams)
After: 15.55 ounces (441 grams)

I also modified my ENO hammock with a different suspension than what it came with.

My new suspension is made from Amsteel, which is ultra-light and super strong. On the hammockforums.net site, you can learn a ton of DIY ideas. You can learn how to make your own stoves, which I discussed earlier, as well as hammocks. They are so much lighter than some of the other hammock brands out there, and if you are handy with a sewing machine, you can make your own. Your own bug net and rain fly.

Making a hammock is as easy as cutting the length of fabric needed and sewing in a hem. Then gather the ends and add your suspension.

Use either some rope, or other cordage, or you can make the suspension out of Amsteel in the form of Whoopie Slings. I don't recommend paracord. Paracord stretches, and you may find yourself waking up on the ground; 550 cord has many uses while backpacking, but using 550 as a suspension might not work for you. In one of the first hammocks I made, I used 550 cord, and it did stretch overnight—not by much in that I did not hit the ground, but it still stretched. I would use Amsteel.

Go to www.hammockforums.net and lurk around a while, and you will find many ideas, tips, and projects for DIY. Look me up if you decide to go there. My user name is GaHammockGuy.

Making your own gear will give you such a great feeling of satisfaction that you made it all by yourself.

# CHAPTER THIRTEEN

# SHARE THE LOAD

On some of your longer trips with more than two hikers, you may want to share the load. You can decide when to share the load and with how many hikers. This is a huge step and the easiest one, so we don't really need to spend a lot of time here.

Most of us want to use our own gear that we made or bought or inherited, but let's think about this for a while. Three hikers do not need to take three stoves, three canisters of fuel, three water filters, or three lighters. You get it? If you have a tent, there are ways to share that load as well. Take one of these items, and you can even combine all the food into one bag, all of the meals, that is. Keep the snacks in one pack and the food that is to be cooked in another bag. Here is how that might work.

If you are the hiker who is carrying the meals, then you will carry the stove and the fuel. If you are carrying the snacks, you will not carry any other food.

If there is a tent on the scene, and three hikers will be sharing the tent, then one hiker will carry the tent, someone else will carry the tent poles, and someone else will carry the rain fly. Those three will be sleeping in the tent, and they will need to stay together. The easiest way to split this up is to plan right so you will all be able to pack light and still carry similar weights in your packs.

When sharing the load, all hikers need to know what each item weighs in said pack. Once you know what each item weighs, you will be able to get with the others in your group who, hopefully, have been counting their ounces, and you can decide who takes what so that each person is carrying the same amount of weight—or close enough to the same amount.

You may be able to shave a few pounds of weight off each of the packs should you decide to split up the gear. A few pounds shaved is a sore back saved!

On one trip, we had seven hikers and six stoves. We had plenty of fuel and food, and since we slept in a shelter on the Appalachian Trail, no tents or hammocks were taken, so there was some shaved weight there, but we all carried our own food. I'm sad to say that not a lot of planning was done on that trip. Had we gotten together sooner and known each other's weight, we all might have taken less. This was prior to my starting down my path to Gram Weenieism, so I learned quite a bit on that trip. We had a blast nonetheless.

To answer the question posed a while back: How do you and when do you start culling items from your pack and decide not to take certain items over others? Now that you have gone on a trip and are back home, it is time to go through the three-pile process.

# CHAPTER FOURTEEN

# THREE-PILE PROCESS

The next step is done at the end of your trip once you are back home, but you might find that you will take this step over and over again.

I spend weeks preparing for a trip. If I know I have one planned for the last weekend in November, I will start putting my pack together during the first week of November. I will pack and unpack, weigh the items, and pack again. Then, I unpack it all, and pack again. This helps me know that I have everything I will need for the trip and helps me practice where it all goes in the pack, which keeps me organized on the trail. I keep packing it all in the same place, and this process just helps me to do so. My wife goes crazy during this time because I have it all upstairs in the living room.

Then during the trip, each morning, when we break camp to go to the next stop, all the items go into the pack the same way, in the same pockets. Remember Chapter Ten? Because I practiced this packing and unpacking ritual, I remember where everything goes.

The three-pile process comes into play after each trip. Once I return home, I take a much-needed shower (per my wife's standing order), then after the shower, I get a good night's sleep. Once I have recovered from the trip, I start to unpack all my gear, usually that following weekend.

As I unpack, I make three piles. This is when I start culling items from my pack, if there are any items that need culling. I will spread out my tarp, and then I start unpacking. For each item I grab, I ask myself one simple, easy-to-answer question. My answer will determine which pile I will use for that item.

How often did I use this item?

- A lot?
- Hardly at all?
- Never?

## *Pile One*

Pile one has all the gear that I used a lot—basically multiple times a day.

Obviously, I would put my hammock and sleeping bag in this pile even though I only used it once a day. The thing is, that when I did use this item, I used it for hours at a time while I slept or rested. I also add to the pile my water filter, cooking pot, and so on. These are items that I can't possibly survive without, even though I used them only once or twice a day during the trip.

Other items that would go into this pile are my fire kit, personal kit, knife, hat, gloves. Trekking poles, the pack itself, and even my sunglasses, all go into pile one.

Remember, this pile is where you will put items that were actually used during the trip.

## *Pile Two*

In this pile, I will put all the gear that I seldom used. I usually don't have too many items in this pile anymore, but starting out, I would put in my plastic trowel. I would also put uneaten food here because I might have taken seven trail bars but eaten only five. On the next trip, I would take five trail bars because I remembered what I put in pile two on the previous trip.

After enough trips, you will find that you will be able to plan your food supply so well that by the time you reach the parking lot at the end of a trip, you will have already eaten all the food. I have actually gotten my snack bag planned so well, that I have eaten my last candy bar at the truck while we were loading it up to start back home. For me, that is smart planning and good organization.

I have a long length of 550 paracord tied up into what looks like a donut.

To follow the three-pile process to the letter, many items, like my paracord donut, would end up in this pile because I only used it one day and only once that day during the entire trip.

## Pile Three

This pile is for the items that you absolutely did not use at all, at any time, during the entire trip. Items like your extra batteries, extra socks, and the game camera.

Okay, let me explain that one. On some trips years ago, I would hear Bigfoot stomping around in camp, so I started taking the game camera when we would car camp. This bad little habit fell over into my backpacking trips as well, because it only weighed 1 pound 8 1/4 ounces. It ended up in pile three and was eventually culled from the pack.

Some other items that may go into this pile are extra bandanas, my DIY wood saw, compact radio, water bag (sometimes I would take extra water bags "just in case"), bug spray, sunscreen, too many fire-starter items, my compass, and even my first-aid kit and multi-tool.

Although I did *not* use my first-aid kit, as little as it was at the time, I still put it in pile three because I want to follow this process to the letter.

At some point, other items that ended up in pile three were extra clothes, like my insulation layers.

On the trips when the forecast called for very cold weather, we planned on it being even colder up on the mountain, so I would overpack the thicker items of clothing. I have gotten better and have culled some clothes and/or replaced them with clothes that are lighter and have less bulk. You might want to go back and review Chapter Eight. At some point those items ended up in pile three. I do not put uneaten food in pile three because I kept the food in my food bag, and I did hit the food bag, every day.

So now all your items should be in one of the three piles. Good job here. Now, what to do with each item?

## Culling Items

Start with pile two, take the items that you seldom used, and ask yourself, "Did I really need to take this item?" If you answered yes, put that item in pile one.

The length of paracord, for instance, always starts in pile two because I only touched this item a time or two, but I must have it, so I put it in pile one during this part of the process. To follow the rules, however, the donut starts out in pile two.

You may have used the plastic trowel only once, but you can use a tent stake to dig a hole if necessary. So put the trowel in pile three because you are now learning how to look at items within your pack as dual-purpose items.

Do this with every item in pile two. Pick an item and decide if you really must have it. If you do, then put it in pile one. Pick another item, ask the same question, and if you don't really need it, put it in pile three. Do this for each item until pile two is gone. Take all the items in pile one and put them back in your gear closet so you can take them on your next trip. Take all the items in pile three and absorb them back into your life at home. Do not plan to take those items again because you already asked yourself if you really needed the items, and you told yourself "No."

If you follow this process to the letter, as I do on each trip, you should not have a pile three after enough trips.

Here's a secret: I always have a pile three after each trip—even if I have only an item or two. If after your next trip you still have a pile three, don't be too rough on yourself. It happens to the best of us.

We want to have fun on our trips, so we tend to take items with us that are fun but not really needed, which is human nature. But these items take up space and add weight, so just decide what you really really really need on a trip. Look back at Chapter Five to review the list to help with your decision.

Good luck and let me know how your progress is going. I hope you get a lighter pack.

# CHAPTER FIFTEEN

# STRENGTH TRAINING

A guy once told me that if you want to lighten your pack, lose some weight. When he saw the puzzled look on my face, he explained a bit further. I was a few pounds overweight and needed to lose some weight—and still do. If you are a few pounds overweight, start working out and lighten some of your own personal weight.

It made sense to me to lose some weight, but pounds instead of ounces, and he was right. The trip will be easier on your knees and back just as it will be with carrying a lighter pack.

Cardio is a great way to burn calories. Run or even walk around the neighborhood a few times a day, or a couple of times a week. Stretching and yoga are other activities that can help. When I am not healing from surgery, I work out using the P90X program, and built into the program is an hour and a half of yoga. It makes me sweat more than the kickboxing portion.

Working out with weights and doing the heavy lifting to rip your muscles is another way to burn fuel. As your muscles heal, it takes protein to fuel the healing process. I dropped about twenty-five pounds with P90X in about three months, and I ate more than I have in my life.

Therefore, if weight training is the path you take, check with your doctor to get recommendations on your limitations and such. Watch what you eat while here in civilization, and remember you can't eat here what you eat on the trail, unless your life, here in civilization, has you walking ten-plus miles every day.

Shaving weight from your pack is as easy as looking at your pack differently. I have enjoyed sharing my thoughts with you, and I hope this book helps with converting you to a Gram Weenie.

# CLOSING

Making the decision to become a Gram Weenie is not a small step. This decision will force you to look at your gear from a different perspective—a perspective that may go against other training you may have gone through. This is why, if you decide to convert to Gram Weenieism, mocking and ridicule may be in your future. I know that, should you go down this path, you will succeed with reducing the weight of your pack. Think about what you are trying to accomplish here.

You are shaving ounces from your pack—a little bit at a time. Each ounce you shave from your pack is one step closer to losing a pound. As a Gram Weenie, you are trying to lose weight an ounce at a time, not one, two, or even three pounds all at once.

I would love to hear how your journey to becoming a Gram Weenie is going, so look me up at www.swlowe.com or email me at steve@swlowe.com.

See you on the trail!

# ABOUT STEVE

Steve is currently living in Atlanta, Georgia, with his lovely wife and has a real passion for the wilderness. Steve has been camping for longer than he can remember. He would go camping with his family at a very young age in a pop-up camper, then with his father in an old Volkswagen bus. He has traveled and camped in RVs as well as tents.

Since then, he has graduated to backpacking with friends in the wilderness, and he hits the trail as often as possible. Over the years, he has researched and tested ways of lightening his pack. This long-time search has turned him into a Gram Weenie, and he has become obsessed with obtaining the lightest pack possible.

Check him out at www.swlowe.com.